AUM

Indian Scriptures

Vedic Literature and Hindu Religion

Prof. Shrikant Prasoon

HINDOOLOGY BOOKS

Published by

HINDOOLOGY BOOKS

An Imprint of

Pustak Mahal®, Delhi

J-3/16 , Daryaganj, New Delhi-110002

☎ 23276539, 23272783, 23272784 • *Fax:* 011-23260518

E-mail: info@pustakmahal.com • *Website:* www.pustakmahal.com

London Office

51, Severn Crescents, Slough, Berkshire, SL 38 UU, England

E-mail: pustakmahaluk@pustakmahal.com

Sales Centre

10-B, Netaji Subhash Marg, Daryaganj, New Delhi-110002

☎ 23268292, 23268293, 23279900 • *Fax:* 011-23280567

Branch Offices

Bangalore: ☎ 22234025

E-mail: pmblr@sancharnet.in • pustak@sancharnet.in

Mumbai: ☎ 22010941

E-mail: rapidex@bom5.vsnl.net.in

Patna: ☎ 3094193 • *Telefax:* 0612-2302719

E-mail: rapidexptn@rediffmail.com

Hyderabad: *Telefax:* 040-24737290

E-mail: pustakmahalhyd@yahoo.co.in

ISBN 978-81-223-1007-8

Edition : January 2008

Printed at : Param Offsetters, Okhla, New Delhi-110020

Dedication

Dedicated to
my guardian and guru
Prof. Ramashraya Prasad Singh,
retired Professor and
Head of the Deptt. (Hindi)
M.S. College, Motihari,
who constantly brought me closer
to the scriptures
throughout the last 45 years,
and to those who need it the most

Preface

Only ã has been taken from scriptural transliteration for long 'a' sound which is otherwise impossible to write in the Roman script. Rest of everything is as written in government papers, magazines, newspapers and general books. It will help in easy reading of the *mantras* and *slokas* quoted in it and also the names of numerous books.

All the general information and vital statistics have been given at their proper places which will give an idea of and an insight into the scriptures from India, which are the **Words of Brahman** and the blessings of our ancient *rishis* to the human beings, whose richness gives **'fullness'**, **'happiness'**, **'purity'**, **'divinity'** and **'bliss'** to all.

While separately introducing the different *Smritis,* I have deliberately and purposely not mentioned them in other chapters so as to be able to cover many different topics in this small book.

Shri Ram Avtar Gupta, the Managing Director of Pustak Mahal, New Delhi, is to be congratulated for planning such books of great importance for the 'ignorant and not-so-ignorant masses', under the Hindoology series, which will definitely bring the readers closer to the rich and divine knowledge and to inner spiritual self. These scriptures are to be followed for health, happiness and prosperity.

HARI AUM TATSAT !

— Prof. Shrikant Prasoon

Contents

Prayers

ॐ पूर्णमदः पूर्णमिदं पूर्णात् पूर्णमुदच्यते।
पूर्णस्य पूर्णमादाय पूर्णमेवावशिष्यते।।
ॐ शान्तिः शान्तिः शान्तिः

Aum purnamadah purnamidam purnāt purnamudachyate
Purnasya purnamādāya purnamewavashishyate
Aum shāntih shāntih shāntih

Aum, the *Sachidānandghan*, the Divine *Brahman*, the Perfect is always perfect from all points of view. The Universe is also complete and perfect because of Him as this perfection has been derived out of that Perfect. The Universe is perfect because of His perfection.

Vedas, the eternal source of knowledge are perfect. Perfect knowledge of *'one', 'some'* or *'many'* can be taken out of it, yet it will remain perfect. Thus both will remain perfect.

It is really wonderful that one perfect tree comes out of one perfect seed and again that tree yields many such perfect seeds for many more perfect trees; and thus the continuity is maintained. Perfection yields perfection. Such is the system behind the creation and the creation has sustained this system so far. If man refrains from interfering into that eternal system, it may continue and grow for billions of years to come.

ॐ विश्वानि देव सवितर्दुरितानि परासुव
यद् भद्रं तन्न आसुव

Aum vishwānideva savitarduritāni parāsuva
yed bhadram tanna āsuva

(O God, keep everything bad and impure away from me, and bring everything good and pure to me.)

OO

1

Hinduism —The Eternal Religion

At the time when divine knowledge came to the *rishis* as revelations or dictates of the Supreme *Brahman* there was no mention of Hindus or Hinduism. So, it is always called *'Sanātan Dharma'* which has come to become a synonym for Hinduism. This '**Eternal religion**' is common and adoptable to every religion. It is the basis of all religions.

वेदोऽखिलो धर्ममूलम्

Vedo akhilo Dharmamulam

Essence of Hinduism

One should never be misguided by any misconception which may have entered one's mind because of the divisions and partitions among human beings. Hinduism is for all human beings as it has declared **Universal Brotherhood** to be its fundamental principle. The Vedas are the seeds and the roots of all the religions. They are universal and infinite. They are the living spirits which are somehow present in every religion. Of course, except Hinduism or *Sanātan Dharma* which is the Eternal Religion, all other religions have knowingly or unknowingly taken only such selected parts which they liked or which were congenial to their needs and thinking. Only the *rishis* were able to see the inner truth and reality and to explain the intricacies. The *rishis* declared that Vedas were perfect but it was not the end. Something more was yet to come.

At a much later stage, Hinduism developed out of Vedas. The people of India accepted them as their integral part, part and parcel of their worldly and spiritual being, of their *Sanātan Dharma*, the Eternal Religion. Hindus and Hinduism were the terms which were used for Indians and their religion respectively by attackers and travellers from other countries. These terms came into existence many millenniums after the *avataran* (arrival) of Vedas and Vedic knowledge.

The Vedas

Veda is the physical presentation of the word *Brahman*. Veda has come out of the etymological root ***'vid'*** which means knowledge. Vedas have four qualities : *sattā* (existence), *jnāna* (wisdom), *vichār* (thought) and *lābh* (gain). Vedas are *vid sattāyām, vid jnāna, vid vichārane* and *vidrilābhe.* They have come out of the breath of the *Brahman* (*yasya niwāsitam vedāh*). Thus, the Vedas are the books of human knowledge (not Hindu knowledge). It is a fact and should be accepted gladly that the total Vedic literature is the root and basis of not only the religions of the world but of human knowledge as well. They are the divine gifts for they are the utterances of the God, which were later seen as vision and repeated by the *rishis*. Broadly speaking they were divided in two categories: *Shrutis* and *Smritis*. Both of them were further divided into different sub-organs (*ang* and *upāng*) by the only Brahmarishi **Krishna Dwaipāyan Ved Vyās.** He was fondly called Ved Vyās for he was the only one who was able to edit and arrange the Vedic knowledge.

All the *Shrutis* and *Smritis* are the orders of *Brahman* which have been stated in the *Bādhoolsmriti* : "*Shrutismriti mamaiwāgye*" (*Shrutis* and *Smritis* are my orders). The word *āgya* has a synonym in *Shāstra* which is defined as "*Nideshgranthayoh shāstram*" — it means the classical treatises which give directions are called *Shāstras*. Maharshi Parashar has said that whatever orders the *Brahman* has given us are not only for us but for the whole Universe. One thing must be seen as a deliberate attempt and not simply a coincidence that the scriptures of every religion of the world are the 'words of their Supreme Lord' in keeping with the '*Brahman Vānee*' as envisaged and claimed about in these eternal scriptures. It is indirectly an assertion that all the religions have their roots in the Vedic knowledge. Here two other points must be considered and always kept in conscious and functional memory. The first one is that the Vedas are endless, *anantā wai vedah,* and the other one is the four different adjectives used in *Manusmriti* for the Vedas:

त्वमेको ह्यस्य सर्वस्य विधानस्य स्वयम्भुवः।
अचिन्त्यस्याप्रमेयस्य कार्यतत्त्वर्थवित् प्रभो।।

Twameko hyasya sarbasya vidhānsya swayambhuvah
Achintyasyāprameasya karyatatwārthavit prabho

– *Manusmriti* (1:3)

The first adjective is ***asya sarbasya*** meaning it is all. Some of it is known as *Shruti* and the rest of the unheard truth is to be known through *Smritis.*

The second adjective is ***swayambhuvah*** meaning self-born, born from the self or will. The *Skanda Purana* also claims that Vedas are physical forms of Narayana ***'Vedo Nārāyanah sākshāt'***. Vedas are not the creation of any human being.

The third adjective is ***achintyasya***, which means that there is no end of the branches of Vedas. 4524 are only the branches of the *Samhitās*. Of course, only a few of them are available, but that does not mean that they can be counted. This book aims at introducing all of those we know.

The fourth adjective for the Vedas is ***aprameasya.*** The meaning is very clear — we cannot understand the Vedas on our own. We must take the help of a blessed Guru, *Meemãnsã*, *Nirukta*, *Purãna* and other Treatises.

At the outset we will have to make it clear in our mind that not only the four known Vedas but all the Hindu scriptures are Vedas, the knowledge. What we know as the four Vedas are, in fact, the *Samhitãs* the collection or anthologies of only the *mantras*. They are a part of the whole Vedas which comprise myriads of known-unknown, available-not available *Granthas*. The *Samhitã* means law, rule, sequential recitation of *mantras* or their pronunciation according to its different divisions: *Varnãnãmatishayitah sannidhih samhitã sangyah syãta*.

Ved Vyãs collected, edited, made different anthologies and categories of the Vedas which is the secondary aim behind this book. The prime aim is to take out, introduce and present the Hindu Scriptures or the *Dharmagranthas* as far as possible and practicable under different limitations both physical and mental, spiritual and religious and of course, the limitations of both the pages and knowledge. These things are so vast and varied that it will take many centuries and many births for a man like me to have 'some' real knowledge of them. That is one of the reasons that many commentaries were written on them by so many saints, sages, teachers and scholars yet they have not been understood fully. Surprisingly enough, most of them have spent their lives in trying to elucidate only a part of it.

So, *Shrutis* are the scriptures in broader sense while only the *Granthas* (Treatises) under the subhead *Smriti* are *Dharmagranthas*, real scriptures of the Hindus, on which all our religious rites and rituals are based. Most of the scriptures of Hinduism are based on the *Smritis* which are not just a different section and division of Vedic knowledge, but an integral part of Vedas and Vedic *Vangmai* (world). They are *Karma Kand,* religious rites and rituals, that are followed in everyday life and worshipping. As the *Brahman* cannot remain confined to one self or one entity, so the Vedas too cannot remain confined to one part only. It is there and everywhere as *Karma* (action) also has vast or infinite connotations.

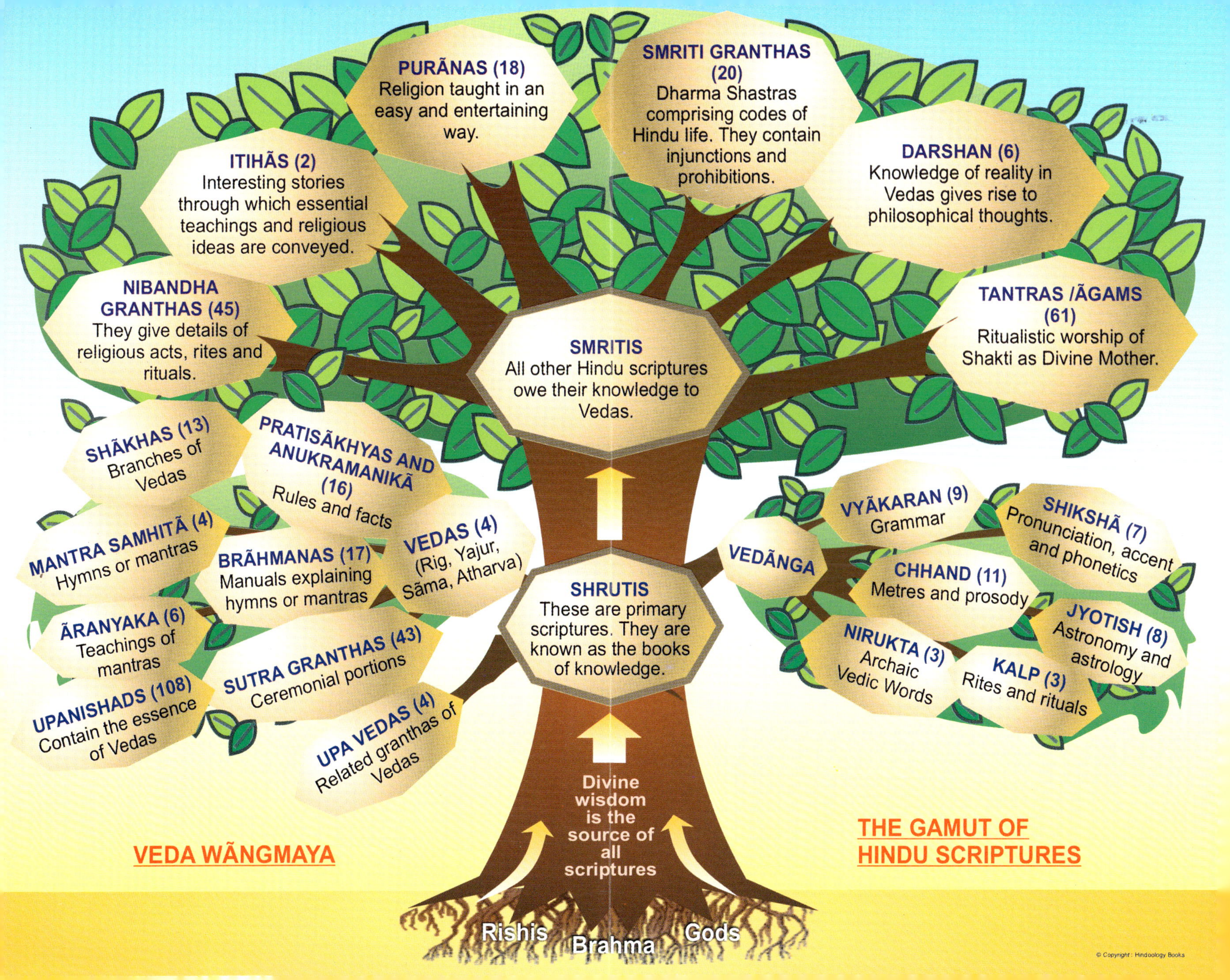
PURĀNAS (18)
Religion taught in an easy and entertaining way.
SMRITI GRANTHAS (20)
Dharma Shastras comprising codes of Hindu life. They contain injunctions and prohibitions.
ITIHĀS (2)
Interesting stories through which essential teachings and religious ideas are conveyed.
DARSHAN (6)
Knowledge of reality in Vedas gives rise to philosophical thoughts.
NIBANDHA GRANTHAS (45)
They give details of religious acts, rites and rituals.
TANTRAS /ĀGAMS (61)
Ritualistic worship of Shakti as Divine Mother.
SMRITIS
All other Hindu scriptures owe their knowledge to Vedas.
SHĀKHAS (13)
Branches of Vedas
PRATISĀKHYAS AND ANUKRAMANIKĀ (16)
Rules and facts
MANTRA SAMHITĀ (4)
Hymns or mantras
BRĀHMANAS (17)
Manuals explaining hymns or mantras
VEDAS (4)
(Rig, Yajur, Sāma, Atharva)
ĀRANYAKA (6)
Teachings of mantras
SUTRA GRANTHAS (43)
Ceremonial portions
UPANISHADS (108)
Contain the essence of Vedas
UPA VEDAS (4)
Related granthas of Vedas
SHRUTIS
These are primary scriptures. They are known as the books of knowledge.
VEDĀNGA
VYĀKARAN (9)
Grammar
SHIKSHĀ (7)
Pronunciation, accent and phonetics
CHHAND (11)
Metres and prosody
JYOTISH (8)
Astronomy and astrology
NIRUKTA (3)
Archaic Vedic Words
KALP (3)
Rites and rituals
Divine wisdom is the source of all scriptures
Rishis
Brahma
Gods
VEDA WĀNGMAYA
THE GAMUT OF HINDU SCRIPTURES
© Copyright : Hindoology Books

2

Introduction to Scriptures

Scriptures are the holy books of a religion, pious and revered. The words of scriptures are said and accepted to be the words of the God, and followed by the followers of that religion faithfully, honestly, diligently and sincerely for health, pleasure, happiness, prosperity, progress and salvation. Every religion of the world has one scripture while Hinduism has many scriptures. Hindus treat all the precious 'Books of Knowledge' as their scriptures, which are like their God, guide and guru.

Scriptures are the books of RELIGION. They teach us to differentiate between religious and irreligious deeds. All the scriptures say that those who lead a religious life, live full and well.

यतो धर्मस्य ततो जय।

Yato dharmasya tato jaya

– *Mahābhārata, Bhishma Parva* (21:11)

(Where there is religion, there is victory.)

To be religious is to live in light; to be irreligious is to live in darkness, to feel pain, to be aggrieved and to die after intense physical and mental suffering or at an early age by accident. It is a hell even among plenty.

Religion

Religion is very wide, large and powerful. It possesses all and can lead one to peace, prosperity and happiness while irreligious habits like immoral sex, power, anger and lust destroy everything good and pleasant, and ultimately result into untold and deeply-felt agony. Hence the scriptures are essential to make our religious and pious duties clear and proclaim what we should do, what we should not, what is allowed and what is not.

Following the teachings of the *Mahābhārata*, all the religions teach good qualities and paths as religious. They distinguish between religious and irreligious deeds and ask to follow only the religious ones:

Religious	Irreligious
1. Love	Anger
2. Truth	Falsehood
3. Equality	Hatred
4. Sharing material wealth	Hiding material wealth

5. Monogamy	Multiple immoral relations
6. Piety	Deceitfulness
7. Simplicity	Luxury
8. Fostering the weak	Selfishness
9. Kindness	Cruelty

These nine religious qualities have been treated as general qualities to be followed by each human being:

अक्रोधः सत्यवचनं संविभागः क्षमा तथा।
प्रजनः स्वेषु दारेषु शौचमद्रोह एव च।।
आर्जवं भृत्यभरणं नवैते सार्ववर्णिकाः।

Akrodhah satyabachanam sambibhāgah chhamā tathā
Prajanah sweshu dāreshu shauchamadroh yeva cha
Ārjawam bhrityabharanam nawaite sārvavarnikā

– *Mahabharata, Shanti Parva* (60:7-8)

Religion is to be natural, to follow natural instincts and to perform all natural activities. As heat and energy is natural to the Sun and burning is to fire so one should work according to one's natural duties with one and only one intention to ensure the continuity of life on the Earth by keeping everything clean and by helping all living beings to grow and prosper. If such religious paths are followed then there will be no war, struggle, strife or robbing others of life, joy or wealth. Only then the Earth would be treated as our true home, where all the living creatures are in unison and the most needed universal brotherhood *'Vasudhaiva Kutumbakam'* (वसुधैव कुटुम्बकम्) can be established. Only then we can pray for the prosperity of all:

सर्वे भवन्तु सुखिनः सर्वे सन्तु निरामयाः।
सर्वे भद्राणि पश्यन्तु मा कश्चिद् दुःखभाग्भवेत्।।

Sarvebhawantu sukhinah sarvesantu nirāmayā
Sarve bhdrāni pashyantu mā kashchid dukhbhāgbhawet

Man must follow only one religion, i.e. human religion, which is the universal religion. Those who wish to get peace, prosperity and to ensure the continuity of life on the Mother Earth must follow and propagate human religion. Each one will grow if human religion is established. Hence religion must exist for the existence of 'all' because progress is made only through religion, while irreligious acts diminish everthing:

धर्मे वर्धति वर्धन्ते सर्वभूतानि सर्वदा।
तस्मिन हर्षति ह्यन्ते तस्मात् धमं ना लोपयेत।।

Dharme bardhati bardhante sarbabhutāni sarbadā
Tasmin harasati hriyante tasmāt dhamam nā lopayet

Ten attributes are the most needed aspects of a human life. When these qualities were found in abundance, man made steady progress in the lap of nature, but when the lust and luxury saw an upsurge in man's life, the natural resources were vehemently and recklessly utilised and destroyed and life Elements were polluted. As a result, the very life and existence is now under threat and the extinction of life is at bay because the greenhouse effect is growing and the hole in the ozone layer has widened up to 73 million kilometres. These are the ten qualities which every human being must adopt for the survival and continuation of life:

Dhriti (firmness), ***chhamā*** (forgiveness), ***dayā*** (kindness), ***asteyam*** (not stealing other's property), ***shaucham*** (purification), ***indriyanigrah*** (self-restraint), ***dhi*** (wisdom), ***vidya*** (knowledge), ***satyam*** (truthfulness), ***akrodho*** (lack of anger).

Importance of Religion

Religion and the scriptures are the most needed and revered possessions. It is claimed that 'religion is the fundamental basis of the Universe' in the sense that all apparently living and non-living things do what they can and because they 'do' hence the universe exists and grows:

Dharmo vishwasya jagatah pratistha

Since the Sun gives light and energy, the air helps in breathing and water supplies the needed liquid so the world exists. Naturally ***"Vishwam dharma pratishtham"*** — the Universe is in the religion. So, by setting religion aside one will die ***"Na dharmam tyajeta jiwitasyapi hetoh."*** The natural, eternal and common for all religion is well defined, explained and laid clearly by Brahmarishi Ved Vyās who says "Because it possesses all, so it is religion. Despite the force and energy of each individual living being, the religion possesses each of them for non-violent co-existence and compassion. Religion teaches the theory of live and let others live. The great men of religion have declared that, anything which is non-violent, is religion. Religion is taught for the growth, progress and existence of living beings on the Earth." So, that which acts with such aim is religious:

धारणाद् धर्ममित्याहु: धर्मो धारयते प्रजा:।
यत् स्याद् धारणसंयुक्तं स धर्म इति निश्चय:।।
अहिंसार्थाय भूतानां धर्मप्रवचनं कृतम्।
य: स्यादहिंसासम्पृक्त: स धर्म इति निश्चय:।।
प्रभवार्थाय भूतानां धर्म प्रवचनं कृतम्।

Dhārnād dharmamityahu dharmo dhāryate prajāh
Yat syād dhāran sanyuktam sa dharma iti nischayah
Ahimsārthāya bhutānām dharmapravachanam kritam
Yeh syād himsā sampriktah sa dharma iti nischayah
Prabhāwārthāya bhutānām dharmapravachanam kritam

According to Bhishma Pitamah, not to be angry, speaking the truth, to share the wealth, getting children from one's own wife, to be pure, not to revolt, being simple and feed worthy of feeding, are the nine general religious duties to be followed by the people of all **Varnas.**

A part of this human religion can keep one free from great fear:

स्वल्पमस्य धर्मस्य त्रायतो महतो भयात।

Swalpamasya dharmasya trāyato mahato bhayāt

That which helps in the growth, development and the prosperity is known as religion. What is the man doing at present? Everything that science has created, like after the invention of automatic machines, weapons for mass destruction and nuclear weapons, which have helped in the establishment of the factories and running the vehicles have continuously destroyed life on the Earth. Man is not willing to work with his own hands (physical power) and mind (mental power), he is totally dependent (rather has surrendered to) on machines which are destroying and polluting everything essential for life. Man is claimed to be the best creation, who is now proving beyond doubt to be the worst creature simply because man today neither has faith in God, nor follows any religion, nor is ready to control his senses, nor works with sense. All animals contribute something to the ecology. It is only man who cannot help in maintaining ecological balance. On the other hand, man has been incessantly, knowingly and vehemently destroying ecology, animals, plants, atmosphere, air, water, ozone, exosphere with numerous poisons and countless other means.

Religious and pious wholesome deeds are self-proved. They need no proof. They should not be discussed or advocated. They should be followed both wisely and blindly. One class of an animal or a plant has one similar religion. Man is also an individual class of animal. Man has wrongly divided himself into different classes, (more for controlling the natural riches and resources). One should never forget that man is **'One Class'**. Man must follow **'One Eternal Human Religion'**.

In place of dedicating ourselves to the books of real knowledge, which make us worldly wise and spiritually alert, we are giving a lot of precious time to other languages and books which give only information and no knowledge.

Uniqueness of Indian Scriptures

One great difference between books of the other parts of the world and the Indian books is that while other books are general books of basic information and entertainment, the Indian books, particularly books in Sanskrit are the books of knowledge and wisdom, they include all arts and all sciences. They give meaning at many layers which we have not been able to decipher as yet.

Indian books also include mythology. While the myths and mythology of other countries, shrouded with disbelief and falsehood, deal with the physical realities, the Indian myths are spiritual in nature and percept and are based on inner and subtle truth and faith.

The scriptures of Hindus are the treatises under the subhead *Smritis*. Even those *Smriti-granthas* are numerous. One hundred *Smriti-granthas* are still available, out of which nine are treated as very important and used in rituals and daily life. They definitely influenced the life and deeds during the medieval period, hence, they are in the limelight. But one thing is guaranteed that not a single living Hindu has seen those available *Smriti-granthas*. Most of the Hindus have seen only the *Manusmriti*, which is easily available. There is another astounding fact that only around 5% of Hindus possess *Manusmriti* and have partially or fully read it. There are hundreds of smaller books compiled, edited and printed out of the *Smritis* (and some from *Puranas*) that are used and followed at the time of some religious rites and rituals. They are very popular and available everywhere. They are the guides.

On the other hand, the scriptures in India are almost countless. No one has a complete list of them. People do not need them. They are dependent on the *pandits* (local priests) who keep only selected books on the popular rituals in their area and spend their whole life in using them repeatedly. They too are not interested in searching out other books and trying to enrich the mind, life and rituals.

These scriptures proclaim and propagate so many rituals and rites that one man cannot perform them during his life time even if he devotes all his life to it. Moreover, they are varied and divided into many ways for different purposes. That is the reason why religion in India is so vivid, varied, colourful and lively. The variations keep the options clear. So, anyone can go for some religious rituals and worship in his individual manner. Availability of materials during a particular season and the wishes, needs and capacity of a devotee play a vital role in determining nature and scale of worshipping or *yajna* or rituals. The details always vary. And as they are both mundane and spiritual and suitable for every type of man so they rejuvenate and energise.

Hindu religion is so powerfully rooted in its soil and spread over and integrated to life, living, thinking and being that despite the fact that different attackers, war-mongers, merchants of death and divisive forces have been working against it since the 7th century with the invasions of Arabs, Turks and Huns yet have not been able to uproot it. They could not, for the roots had gone deep and spread all around. They destroyed a lot, but could not obliterate it completely. *Though neither the soil nor the mind has remained the same what it was a hundred years ago, yet divinity and humanity is still there, mixed up with the soil of the land and in the mind of the people.*

The loss is mostly to the world and a bit to Indians for they have the capacity to retain them in their memory *(Smriti)* by listening *(Shruti)*. But the other parts of the world have neither the tradition of *Shruti* or *Smriti*, nor that individual and social teaching and training method which is the best way to carry forward the basic principles of life, living, Nature and cosmos. They cannot know and keep them even partially. The best examples are the NRIs who left India and lost the connection. They too have become materialists and are unhealthy, aggrieved and depressed which is a sure outcome of excessive indulgence into physical pleasure and luxury.

Conclusion

To conclude one can safely say that as those divine books are the basis of all the religions and provide the fundamental base to all religions, naturally they help in creating and shaping the scriptures of other religions. They are the base of Hinduism, and its body and soul too. Their well-defined but undercurrent presence in every religion is another proof that life and civilisation spread all over the world through the people who left this country and went to other parts of the world and because the return journey would have spelled their doom so they settled there. In this way all human beings are brothers and sisters. But this is not the issue in discussion here. It is a matter for the scholars to discuss, and for the men of the other parts of the world to deny. In any case, none is interested in forcing anyone to accept or deny a theory about the time gone by and lived up many millenniums back in the remote past. It simply suggests its universal appeal and importance. But one must look both inside one's heart and mind and outside on the growing pollution and deteriorating living conditions. That is the real challenging problem which each one is facing but no one is ready to mend his ways or do the needful to improve them. In the illusory name of independence, man is steadily growing dependent, facing difficulties, getting restless, and yet not preparing a balance sheet of the material gain on the one side and the loss of life and life-saving elements on the other.

असतो मा सद्गमय।
तमसो मा ज्योतिर्गमय॥

Asato mā sadgamaya
Tamaso mā jyotirgamya

OO

3

Vedas and Shrutis — Books of Knowledge

ONE

Vedas are the mental status and physical forms of Brahman, the Absolute God. Vedas are eternal and invincible. They were breathed out by the Brahman: ***yasya nihswasitam Vedah***. They are the gifts of the Brahman which have been envisioned, collected, compiled, kept and taught by the Rishis and Maharshis after every delusion of the earth. These statements will become crystal clear and what at present seems to be exaggeration will become 'mild' and 'balanced' once the whole world of the Vedas comes to perception.

The very basis and the original pillars of Eternal Religion and Indian Culture and Civilisation are the Vedas. Vedas are the means of both worldly (*laukika*) and spiritual (*alaukika*) knowledge. They appeared in the heart of the first poet Brahmã: *tene Brahmã hridã a ãdikavaye*; and it is believed that they do show at the beginning of every *Kalpa*.

Creation of Vedas

It is believed that Brahmã, the Creator, was born out of the navel of Lord Nãrãyana. He was born out of his self-will so he is said to be *swayambhu*. After birth as he sat on the umbilical cord of the navel-lotus he was unable to move his head and see what was around him. So he started turning his eyeballs around to see. The result was that he got four faces and mouths, one in each direction. From then on he is called *Chaturmukh* (the one with four faces): ***Parikraman vyomni vivrit netrashchatwãri lebhe anudisham mukhãni.***

(परिक्रमन् व्योमनि विवृत नेत्रशचत्वारि लेभे अनुदिशम् मुखानि)

Brahmã could not see a thing. Then, he took *samãdhi*, started meditation and did penance. As a result of his penance he was able to see the Perfect *Purush Nãrãyana*, and on His advice Brahmã resolved to create the Universe. At the insistence of Nãrãyana, the Goddess of Learning, Saraswati, took a seat in the heart of Brahmã. It was then that the *mantras* came out of his mouth. The *mantras* from the eastern mouth became *Rig Veda*, those from the southern mouth became *Yajur Veda*, from the western mouth came out the *Sãma Veda* and from the northern mouth came *Atharva Veda*. Later on he sang the *Upa Vedas* and the *Vedãngs*. The *Itihas* (epics) and *Purãnas* were also recited. Thus everything in the Universe is the creation of Brahmã.

Later, on the request of the gods, Brahmā created *Nitishāstra* which had one lakh chapters and included subjects like *Karma Kānd, Gyāna Kānd, agriculture, commerce, jurisprudence, and political and moral codes.*

Then, what is Veda?

Veda is defined by Sāyanāchārya as following:

इष्ट प्राप्त्य अनिष्ट परिहार लौकिकामुपम।
यो ग्रन्थो वेदयति स वेदः।।

Ishta prāptya anishta parihāra laukikamupām
yo grantho vedayati sa Vedah

(That treatise is called Veda which teaches worldly or spiritual ways and means to get one's desires fulfilled, and to get away from destructive things.)

Since knowledge is infinite so Vedas are also called *anant* (infinite): ***anantā wai Vedāh.***

Manusmriti claims that *Shrutis* are called Vedas: ***shrutistu vedo vigyeyah.***

It is claimed by the *Mahābhārata* that the Creator created the Vedas first, then out of them the world was created: ***Anādinidhanā vidyā vāgutsrishtā swayambhuvā.***

Vedas are treated as invincible: ***apaurusheyam vākyam vedah.***

Vedas are divided into *mantras* and *Brāhman Granthas*: ***mantrabrāhmanyorvedānāmdheyam.***

It has already been established beyond any doubt that the words of Vedas that we see and read and the meaning that we derive are not the real meanings. Vedas give meanings at four different layers. One is for the common people which is called *Vaikhari Vāka*, and the other mysterious three are *Parā Vāka, Pashyanti Vāka* and *Madhyamā Vāka*:

चत्वारि वाक् परिमीता पदानि तानि विदुरब्राह्मणा ये मनीषिनाः।
गुहा त्रीणि निहिता नेनग्यन्ति तुरीयम वाचो मनुष्या वदन्ति।।

Chatwāri vāka parimitā padāni tāni vidurbrāhmanā ye manishināh
Guhā trini nihitā nengyanti turiyam vācho manushyā vadanti

It is written both in *Shatpatha Brāhman* and *Māndukyopanishad* that there are wonderful things and powers hidden in every part and every letter of each word of each *mantra*.

What are they?

Our forefathers had saved some things which the *rishis* had handed over to them. But those illuminated and enlightened minds are not there in the present era that can show, teach or give the other unknown three meanings of the Veda *mantras*. Despite many *Bhāshya* and commentaries, the secret is still undeciphered for the reasons best known to the *rishis*.

TWO

When we say eternal books of knowledge, it carries one sense and our concept is automatically widened; when we say the books of ancient India, somehow it imposes a limitation; when we say the scriptures, we confine them to religion and religious rites; and when we say the scriptures of Hinduism, the boundary gets prominence and the prejudices come to the surface. In that, we lose our magnificence.

The eternal books of Humanism were termed as the books of a sect called Hinduism by those who attacked India in ancient times. They did so because the Indians mostly lived around Indus river which was also known as Sindhu River. This Sindhu changed into Hindu and the supreme books of human knowledge and human religion became the scriptures of Hindus. It all happened because of the prejudices of those people who themselves had taken almost everything from these books of knowledge and converted into their own religion.

Though, Vedas are Human Religion or Eternal Religion but in the modern times, the Vedas and Hinduism are synonymous to each other.

The origin of Hinduism is the Vedas which are the dictates and orders of the Brahman: ***shrutismritimamaiwagya*** (*Shrutis* and *Smritis* are my orders.)

They are human religion. They have divided all the human beings into four classes according to the skill that they acquire and the work that they know and perform. This division is not based on birth. It is based on profession:

i. Wise men are *Brahmins* i.e. from teachers to scientists.

ii. Rulers are *Kshatriyas* i.e. from constables to commanders and from punch to presidents.

iii. Businessmen are *Vaishyas* i.e. from traders to industrialists.

iv. Workers are *Shudras* i.e. the labour class.

Simply because of their birth or the job they hold, they cannot belong to that class. They must possess the ability to successfully, sincerely and honestly fulfil everything that is required from them. Unfortunately, most of the people do not possess the ability and aptitude for the work they are doing. They are not actually fit for their job. They are simply doing that to earn a living; hence they do not belong to that class.

It is a great mix-up in the modern world and modern society. As a result, the performance is not up to the mark and there is a lot of disbelief. The wise blindly follow the rulers and the rulers always try to please a special section that elected them. This happens because the rulers have not been selected on their ability but by the wishes of the electorate.

Life is not an election; it is the whole, a combination of all similar and disparate elements and phenomenon. *No one is honestly, sincerely and wisely fulfilling one's duties. Most of us do not know exactly what we have to do throughout the days and nights. We have 'duty hours' after which we are free to do what we like. Life should not be lived in piecemeal. It is a complete experience. Just like the employment is the duty towards earning, we have duties towards Nature, society, other beings and self.* Life must be taken in broader prospect. We must know the place of life in Nature, Universe, Cosmos and our duties in that setup.

The words of God, as heard and seen by the visionary *rishis* and collected in the *Shrutis* and *Smritis*, are Books of Knowledge. Either we must know them and follow them or we must always do only good to others. None should try to put forward logic to prove himself correct or compare with others. All born on the earth will have to ensure the safety and continuity of life and make living easier, happier and healthier. This is what the Vedas teach and show. One has to see and learn and follow them. **They are the scriptures for all the human beings** and not only for Hindus or those born in a Hindu family or in the family of a *Shudra, Vaishya, Kshatriya* or *Brahmin*.

We start with a wrong and prejudiced concept and waste our lives, the lives of others and Nature at large. We have foolishly brought the earth and the life on it at the brink of total extinction. Under these devastating circumstances, the divine truth and knowledge seen and shown by the *Shrutis* and *Smritis* are very pertinent and important. The truth often obviously appears to be incongruous and unacceptable. **That which soothes the body and pleases the mind is often and directly destructive.** This is the time to choose between the healthier continuation of life or annihilation of life, life elements, the earth and the atmosphere.

Our life, living and dying, is not important; we have to ensure now whether the great-grandson of our great-grandson will take birth or not. We cannot ensure it by accumulating wealth. We can ensure it only by saving Nature, natural phenomenon, natural wealth, and the energy and life on the earth and in the Universe.

For that we will have to turn towards the Books of Knowledge, the scriptures, the Vedas, the *Shrutis* and the *Smritis*, which are basically one and the same thing. Before turning towards them let us first know them.

Three

The Vedas, and for that matter all scriptures, are the whole and have branches. 'The whole' here will bear a continuity and the branches will carry separate identity which will suggest their divisions. The sense of completeness will come out at the end.

It is difficult to give adequate information about all the scriptures in a book of this size. The effort is taken to give a comprehensive list of the books and some important facts about all of them to show their usefulness, and to open the eyes of the readers so that in place of running after one attractive bright and enchanting side of one leaf they can see the whole tree, from the roots to the fruits. Vedas can be broadly known but not in detail. The details may not be there but the whole, its branches, boughs, leaves, flowers and fruits are here full of energetic green pigments.

Some people laugh that the modern *pandits* do not know, how many Vedas are there. Of course, they do not know and they cannot know. Some of them have read only the *Samhitās* which are though just the parts of Vedas but are commonly known and accepted as complete Vedas. The illusion is created when there are ads in papers and magazines about the four known Vedas as 'Complete Vedas'. Vedas are endless. The Creator is their creator. They have not been written by a man. Brahmarishi Ved Vyās only edited and compiled them. The known *Samhitās* are the most popular. We will concentrate mostly on the available scriptures. Though there will be an honest effort to mention the claimed numbers, as far as practicable or the information collected yet it is difficult to mention them with all correctness and confidence.

The Vedas are broadly divided in two groups known as *Shruti* and *Smriti*. *Shrutis* are the books of knowledge: pure sciences, humanities, and cosmological etc while *Smritis* are related to daily works, rituals and rites. They answer the most important question: *What we should do and what we should not do.*

The only difference between the *Shrutis* and the *Smritis* is that the Vedas are the words of God while the *Smritis* are the words of *rishis*. The first one is seen, heard and collected by the *rishis* but the second one is their own thought and analysis, and the remainder of Vedas is in their memory.

Shruti

1. *Vedas* and *Upa-vedas*
2. *Vedāng*

Smriti

1. *Smriti*
2. *Purāna*
3. *Itihās*
4. *Darshan*
5. *Nibandh*
6. *Āgam*

Division of Vedas

The Vedas are further divided into 7 broader divisions.

1. *Mantra Samhitās*
2. *Shākhās*
3. *Brahman Grantha*
4. *Āranyak*
5. *Upanishad*
6. *Sutra Grantha*
7. *Pratisākhya* and *Anukramani*

OO

Four

Vedas

Vedas stand for all the knowledge of man. Veda means knowledge. There is no religion away from the Vedas: ***nā Veda bāhyo dharmah.***

And there is nothing about which the *rishis* have not said something: ***Rishih sarva drashtāh.***

Devapitrimanushyānāma Vedaschakshuh sanātanah or Vedas are the eyes of gods, ancestors and men. Vedas have their use and utility in all the three divisions of time — past, present and future: ***bhutam bhavyam bhavishyam cha sarvam Vedān prasidhyati.***

Vedas are the words of *Brahman*: *shabda Brahman*. The words of Veda contain all. A person who knows Vedas knows everything but the problem is that none can know Vedas well for they are infinite: ***anantah wai Vedah.***

Since it is almost impossible to understand the Original *Mantra Samhitās* known as ***Rig Veda, Sāma Veda, Yajur Veda*** and ***Atharva Veda*** so their Brahmin Divisions are always combined with them because they explain, analyse and elucidate the mantras of the related *Samhitā*.

Initially the Vedas are divided in two groups named *Mantra Samhitās* and *Brahman Granthas*. Without the *Brahman Granthas,* the meaning of the *Mantra Samhitā* cannot be clear. Both the *Mantra Samhitās* and *Brahman Granthas* are called Vedas: ***mantrabrahmnayoh Vedā.***

These *Brahman Granthas* are further divided in two more branches: ***Āranyaka*** and ***Upanishad*** and all these three divisions are known as *Brahman Granthas*. They deal with general knowledge: Cosmology, Astronomy, Materialistic, Spiritual and Divine knowledge. They include Physics, Chemistry, Botany, Zoology and other sciences, and Humanities.

To separate the different subjects from the original *Mantra Samhitās,* ***Vedāng*** were written. The *Vedāng* have six different subjects and hence are divided in six groups:

i. *Shikshā*
ii. *Kalpa*
iii. *Vyakaran*
iv. *Nirukta*
v. *Chhand*
vi. *Jyotish*

For this particular purpose four ***Upa-vedas*** were written. The *Upa-vedas* are:

a. *Arthaveda* (Economy)
b. *Dhanurveda* (Weaponry)
c. *Gandharvaveda* (Music and Fine Arts)
d. *Ayurveda* (Medicine)

Mantra Samhitãs

In fact, there is only one Veda. Maharshi Krishna Dwaipayan or Ved Vyãs first divided them into three which came to be known as *Vedatrayee*, then he added one more and those four divisions of *Mantra Samhitãs* became popular as Four Vedas.

There is yet another view that Ved Vyãs taught these Vedas to his four distinguished disciples: **Paila, Vaishampãyana, Jaimini** and **Sumantu.** Then under his guidance, he asked them to collect these books separately. They became:

1. *Rig Veda*
2. *Yajur Veda*
3. *Sãma Veda*
4. *Atharva Veda*

Because of this division, Maharshi Krishna Dwaipayan came to be known as Brahmarishi Ved Vyãs.

In the *yajna,* there are four *Ritwijs* who sit at the four corners of the *yajna* arena and recite the *mantras*. Each of them represent one particular Veda. The *Ritwij* of *Rig Veda* is called *Hota, Adhwaryu* of *Yajur Veda, Udgãtã* of *Sãma Veda* and the *Ritwij* of *Atharva Veda* is called Brahmã. It seems to be pertinent to mention here that in these scriptures *Brahman, Brãhman* or Brahmin and Brahmã are different words. In Vedas, the ***Chhand***, the metre in which the *mantra* is to be recited, ***rishi***, who saw the *mantra* in *samādhi* (meditation); ***Devatā***, who is referred to in that *mantra* and ***Viniyoga*** of every *mantra* is fixed. The letters cannot change place in a *mantra* while the sequence of both the collection and recitation can change. That is the reason why other *rishis* taught these *mantras* in the way they liked or found fit for teaching. Some of them taught according to the *devatā*, others according to *Chhand* or subject or uses. So, many branches came out of the Vedas.

1. Rig Veda

Rig Veda is definitely the most ancient book written by human beings when the rest of the world knew nothing about writing. It was written on leaves which could be used as paper and ink was made from the plants. It is accepted as such by the whole world.

Rig Veda has its etymology in Sanskrit *ric* (praise) + *veda* (knowledge). Perhaps it is the original Veda when there was only one Veda. So, it is the earliest known Veda.

Rig Veda consists of 1,017 hymns. The number will go up to 1,028 if the apocryphal *Valakhilya* hymns 8.49-8.59 composed in Vedic Sanskrit are included.

The number of the *mantras* or the verses is 10,552. These are contained in 10 books, known as *mandalas*.

This long collection of short hymns is mostly devoted to the praise of the gods. There are certain references to historical events, particularly the struggle between *Āryans*, the early Vedic people and their quite unknown enemies, the *Dasa*.

The chief gods of the *Rig Veda* are:

- *Agni*, the sacrificial fire
- *Indra*, a heroic god who is praised for having slain his enemy Vrtra
- *Soma*, the sacred potion made from soma plant

Other prominent gods are *Mitra, Varuna* and *Ushās* (the dawn). Also invoked are *Savitar, Vishnu, Rudra, Pushān, Brihaspati, Brahmanaspati, Dyaus Pita* (the sky), *Prithivi* (the earth), *Surya* (the sun), *Savitar, Vāyu* (the wind), the *Māruts*, the *Ashvins*, the *Ādityas*, the *Ribhus*, the *Vishvadevas* (all gods) as well as various minor gods, persons, natural phenomena and rivers, trees, animals etc.

It is neither intriguing nor a wonder that some of the names of gods and goddesses praised in *Rig Veda* are also found among other Indo-European people and have been famous since ancient times. They are:

- *Dyaus* is cognate to Greek *Zeus*
- *Mitra* to Persian *Mithra*
- *Ushās* is Greek *Eos*, Latin *Aurora*
- *Agni* corresponds to Latin *Ignis*

This is a proof that Indian people in Vedic times had connections with the people of other places.

The text has been handed down to the posterity since time immemorial or may be since its compilation in two versions: *Samhitāpatha* and *Pādapatha.*

The ***Samhitāpatha*** has all the rules of *sandhi* of Sanskrit language applied and is the text used for recitation.

The ***Pādapatha*** has each word isolated in its pause form and is used for memorisation.

It seems that *Pādapatha* is a commentary to the *Samhitāpatha*, but they may have served an altogether different purpose.

The original text that aims to recover the sacred hymns in the form of their composition by the *rishis*, seems to be somewhere between the two, but closer to the *Samhitāpatha.*

There are ten mandals of *Rig Veda.*

First Mandal (Book 1)

It consists of 191 hymns and 2006 *mantras*. Hymn 1.1 is addressed to Agni, arranged so that the name of this god is the first word of the *Rig Veda*. The remaining hymns are mainly addressed to Agni and Indra. Hymns 1.154 to 1.156 are addressed to Lord Vishnu. The *rishi* of the first *mandal* is Vishwāmitra and Gayatri Chhand has been used in composing the *mantras.*

Second Mandal (Book 2)

It consists of 43 hymns and 429 *mantras* which have been addressed mainly to Agni and Indra. Its *rishi* is Gritasamad and the *mantras* have been composed in Jagati Chhand.

Third Mandal (Book 3)

It contains 62 hymns and 626 *mantras* which address and praise mainly Agni and Indra. Vishwāmitra is the main *rishi* of this *mandal.* The verse 3.62.10 gained great importance in Hinduism as the *Gāyatri Mantra.*

Fourth Mandal (Book 4)

It contains 58 hymns and 589 *mantras* mostly devoted to Agni and Indra. The *rishi* of this *mandal* is Vāmadeva.

Fifth Mandal (Book 5)

It contains 87 hymns and 727 *mantras* mainly dedicated to Agni and Indra, the Vishvadevas, the Maruts, the twin-deity Mitra-Varuna and the Ashvins. Two hymns each are dedicated to Ushas and to Savitar. The main *rishi* of this *mandal* is Ātreya and the Chhand is both *Trishtupa* and *Anushtupa.*

Sixth Mandal (Book 6)

It contains 75 hymns and 765 *mantras* mainly eulogising Agni and Indra. The principal *rishi* is Bharadwāja and the Chhands are mixed: *Anushtupa, Trishtupa, Jagati* and *Gāyatri.*

Seventh Mandal (Book 7)

It contains 104 hymns and 841 *mantras* that are addressed to Agni, Indra, the Vishvadevās, the Māruts, Mitra-Varuna, the Ashvins, Ushā, Indra-Varuna, Varuna, Vāyu, two each to Saraswati and Vishnu, and to others. This *mandal* is famous as the *mandal* of Brahmarishi Vashishtha. He has used mostly *Virāta Chhand* but in 19-25 the *mantras* are in *Trishtupa Chhand.*

Eighth Mandal (Book 8)

There are 103 hymns and 726 verses in this division which have been addressed to different gods. Hymns 8.49 to 8.59 are the apocryphal *valakhilya*, the majority of them are devoted to Indra. Different *rishis* such as Kānva, Medhātithi, Plāyogi, and Rishikā Shashwati Āngirashi have envisioned the *mantras* and have used different Chhands to compose them like *Pragātha*, *Brihati* and *Trishtupa*.

Ninth Mandal (Book 9)

The 114 hymns and 1108 verses are all devoted to *Soma Pavamana*, the plant of the sacred potion of the Vedic religion. It is famous as the *mandal* of Vishwāmitra. Chhands used are *Pankt, Pragātha, Virāt, Brihati, Ushnika, Trishtupa, Jagati* and *Gāyatri.*

Tenth Mandal (Book 10)

With 191 hymns and 1,754 verses or *mantras* the last *mandal* of *Rig Veda* is the biggest division. It is devoted mainly to Agni and Indra but many other gods have also been praised in it. As it is the last division, so all the remaining *rishis* have found place in it. In the West, probably the most celebrated hymns are 10.129 and 10.130 dealing with creation. Especially because they claim that since the learned men were born after the creation, so none can say definitely and correctly about the creation — Whose creation is this? Who created it? How and when was it created? Even the Creator cannot tell it correctly for He was busy in Creation and was absorbed in it:

को अद्धा वेद क इह प्र वोचत् कुत आजाता कुत इयं विसृष्टिः।
अर्वाग्देवा अस्य विसर्जनेनाथा को वेद यत् आबभूव।।

Ko addhā veda ka eh pra wochatkuta ājātā kuta eyam visrishtih
Arwāgdevā asya visarjanenāthā ko veda yata ābabhuva

— *Rig Veda* (10:129:6)

Earlier it was claimed that 22 *suktas* deal with charity but the modern *Vedagya* say that as many as 68 *suktas* praise the charity and the gifts given by the kings. There are 20 *suktas* which show the advent of drama for they are written as dialogues.

Three among them are famous and have been used vehementally by modern writers for plays and poetic creations. They are:

- The dialogue between Pururwā and Urvashi (Rig. 10:85)

- The talk between Yama-Yami (Rig. 10:10)
- The dialogue between Sarmā and Pani

Trishtupa Chhand contains 44 letters, *Gāyatri Chhand* contains 24 *varnas* or letters while *Jagati Chhand* contains 48 letters. These three Chhands have been vehementally used in *Rig Veda.*

According to the Preface written by Vidyādhar Gaud for *Kātyāyan Shrout Sutra, Rig Veda* is divided in 64 chapters; 8 *ashtaks* of 8 chapters each; 10 *mandals* or divisions; 2,006 *varga* (classes); 1000 *suktas*; 85 *anuvāka* (sub-richas); and 10,440 *mantras* or *richas*. Moreover, there are eleven *Bālkhilya Suktas* in it from 43 to 59 in the 8th *mandal.* These are read and recited while in self-study.

There are many famous and important *suktas* in *Rig Veda* which are recited at different times. Most of these *suktas* have been included in *purānas*, particularly *Skandapurāna* and *Padmapurāna*. They are: *Shrisukta, Rātrisukta, Medhāsukta, Shivasankalpsukta* and *Sangyāna Sukta.*

2. Yajur Veda

The Vedas are divided in three forms depending upon their style of composition. These three forms are *ric*, *yajuh* and *sāma*. The Mantras in metrical composition became *Rig Veda,* the collection of prosaic *mantras* was termed *Yajur Veda* and the lyrical songs are famous as *Sāma Veda.*

According to Yāska, the famous writer of *Nirukta*, the word *yajuh* has come out of the root *yaja* (*Nirukta* 7:20). It means that the form of a *yajna* is determined by *Yajur Veda*.

In this way, the *Yajur Veda* is the Veda of sacrificial formulas consisting of archaic prose mantras and also in part of verses borrowed from the *Rig Veda*.

There are two major Branches or recensions of *Yajur Veda* known as the *Krishna (dark) Yajur Veda* and *Shukla (bright) Yajur Veda*. The origin of these branches is very clear. Generally the *mantras* coming from the *Āditya* (Sun) tradition were collected in *Shukla Yajur Veda* while the *mantras* coming from the *Brahman* tradition were collected in *Krishna Yajur Veda*.

It is said that Maharshi Yāgyavalkya, after great penance, received the *Shukla Yajur Veda* from the Sun-God:

आदित्यानिमानि शुक्लानि यांजुषी वाजसनेयेना
याज्ञवल्क्येनाख्यायन्ते।

Ādityānimāni shuklāni yanjushi
Wajasaneyena Yāgyavalkyenākhyāyante

— *Shatpatha Brahman* (14:9:4:33)

The *Shukla Yajur Veda* contains only the verses and sayings necessary for the sacrifice, while explanations exist in a separate *Brahman Granth*. It differs widely from the *Krishna Yajur Veda*, which incorporates such explanations in the work itself, often immediately following the verses. Four major recensions of *Shukla Yajur Veda* survive, all showing by and large the same arrangement, but differing in many other respects, notably in the individual discussion of the rituals, and in the matters of phonology and accent.

There is a very interesting story related to the creation of *Yajur Veda* and its branches, particularly its different names. The incident occurred when the four divisions of the Vedas were completed by Ved Vyās and he had finished teaching Vedas to his famous disciples — Paila, Vaishampāyana, Jaimini and Sumantu.

Vaishampāyana taught *Yajur Veda* to his disciples with right earnestness and great success. From among his disciples, Yāgyavalkya was his favourite because of his diligence and brilliance. But it so happened that somehow he became angry with Yāgyavalkya. Out of anger and in the heat of the moment, he ordered Yāgyavalkya to forsake the knowledge that he had given. Yāgyavalkya had no other option left but to obey his perceptor. With the power of his *yoga* he gave physical form to the abstract *yajus* and threw out all the knowledge given by his guru. These thrown up *yajus* were eaten away by other disciples who took the form of *teetar* bird. From then on, those *yajus* came to be known as *Krishna Yajur Veda*. The disciples who had taken the forms of *teetar* bird came to be known as *taiteriya* which became the name of an *Āranyaka* and an *Upanishad.*

Later Yāgyavalkya became a very famous and accomplished *rishi.* After being humiliated and scrapped up by his guru, the aggrieved disciple went all out for penance in order to please Āditya. He had confidence and devotion. The Sun was pleased with him and one day he came to Yāgyavalkya at noon, in the form of a *bāji* (horse) and taught him the *yajus.* These were called to be *Shukla Yajur Veda*; and because he was taught during the noon hours so another name was given to it *Mādhyāndin* and because the Sun had come in the form of a *bāji* so it was called Vājasneya also. From then on Vājasneya became another name for *rishi* Yāgyavalkya. The Vājasneyi-Mādhyāndin branch of *Yajur Veda* is very popular in North India and Nepal.

Two branches of *Shukla Yajur Veda* are available – *Mādhyāndin* and *Kanva Shākhā.*

The ***Mādhyāndin Shākhā*** has 40 chapters in all and a total of 303 *anuwāks* and 1,975 *kandikās* are there. *Mantras* have been divided into *kandikās* but the *Samhitā* is silent about which *kandikā* has how many *mantras.* 39 chapters out of 40 deal with *Shrout Karma Kanda* in the following order:

- 1st and 2nd chapters deal with *Purnamās* and *Pindpitri yajna.*
- 3rd chapter deals with *Agnihotra.*

- 4th to 8th chapters deal with institutions of *Soma.*
- 9th and 10th chapters deal with *Rājasuya yajna* and *Bājpeya yajna.*
- From 11th to 18th chapters deal with the selection of *Agni.*
- 19th to 21st chapters deal with *Sautrāmani yajna.*
- From 22nd to 25th chapters deal with *Aswamedha yajna* by *Kshatriyas.*
- From 26th to 29th is the collection of *Khilya mantras.*
- 30th to 33rd is the collection of *Purushmedh, Purushsukta* and *Sarvamedh mantras.*
- 34th chapter has *Shivasamkalpa Upanishad.*
- 35th contains *Pitrimedh mantras.*
- From 36th to 39th is the collection of *Pravargya mantras.*
- The last 40th chapter has *Ishāvāshyo Upanishad* which is treated as the best among all the *Upanishads.*

The ***Kānva Shākhā*** is similar to the first in many ways and nowadays it is very popular in Maharashtra, Karnataka, Tamil Nadu, Andhra Pradesh and Orissa. It has 40 chapters. The number of *anuwāks* is 328 and that of the *mantras* is 2,086. The subject matter is the same in both the recensions.

3. Sāma Veda

Ved Vyās taught *Sāma Veda* to Jaimini and from him the tradition of *Sāma Veda* started. Jaimini taught *Sāma Veda* to his son Sumantu and in turn Sumantu taught it to his son Sunwān who taught it to his son Sukarmā. In this way, the long and important tradition of the *Sāma Veda* has continued till date.

Before Jaimini, it was the oral tradition but as it is established beyond doubt that Lord Ganesh wrote the *Māhābhārata* for Ved Vyās so it can be easily concluded that the four famous disciples of Ved Vyās must have written the Vedas and the written tradition must have started from there.

Originally the Vedas were in poetry, prose and lyrics. Lyrics are songs and are sung at the time of offering the *Sāma*. Thus these songs were collected at one place and became the *Sāma Veda*.

At the time of offering the *Sāma*, thirteen *Āchāryās* are mentioned. They are:

1. Rānāyana
2. Sātyamugri Vyāsa
3. Bhāguri Oulund
4. Gaulomulavi
5. Bhānumāna
6. Oupmanyawa

7. Dārāla
8. Gāgarya
9. Sāvarni
10. Vārshagan
11. Kuthumi
12. Shālihotra
13. Jaimini

Out of these thirteen, only three branches of *Sāma Veda* are available nowadays. Nothing is known about the rest of the ten branches.

The available branches are:

- *Rānāyaneeya* by Rānāyana which is popular in Southern countries.
- *Kauthmeeya* by Kuthumi which is studied mostly in the north of the Vindhyāchal.
- *Jaimineeya* by Jaimini which is studied only in Kerala.

The most popular version in India is *Kauthumeeya* Branch. According to the way of singing, there are two popular systems known as *Nāgar* System and *Madra* System. But there is yet another system popular in Varanasi. It is the *Govardhani* System of *Rānāyaneeya* Branch.

The *Sāma Veda* is the 'Veda of chants' or the 'Book of Music' or the 'Knowledge of melodies'. The name of this Veda is taken from the Sanskrit word *Sāma* which means a metrical hymn or song of praise like the word '**Psalm**' in English.

Sāma Veda consists of 1549 stanzas, taken entirely (except 78) from the *Rig Veda*. Some of the *Rig Veda* verses are repeated more than once. Including repetitions, there are a total of 1875 verses included in the *Sāma Veda* recension. Its purpose was liturgical to serve as a songbook for the singer priests who took part in the liturgy. A priest who sings hymns from the *Sāma Veda* during a ritual is called an *Udagātir*, a word derived from the Sanskrit root *ud-gai* 'to sing' or 'to chant'. The styles of chanting are important to the liturgical use of the verses. The hymns were to be sung according to certain fixed melodies, hence the name *Sāma Veda* was given to the collection.

It has been often claimed that there are one thousand branches of *Sāma Veda*. In modern times, some of the scholars of Vedas are extending logic that there were about one thousand systems of pronunciation of the *Sāma mantras*, that is why a thousand branches are claimed.

Jaimini propounded a *sutra Geetishu Sāmākhyā* which established the fact that only songs can be taken as *Sāma mantras*. The *Sāma Veda Mantra Samhitā* contains both *Ārchic* (which is further divided in *Purvārchika* and *Uttarārchika*) and *Gāna*. Both combined together have 27 chapters and 1,875 *mantras*.

Except for the 75 *mantras*, rest of the *mantras* are found in the *Shãkal* branch of *Rig Veda*. But the pronunciations of both *Rig Veda* and *Sãma Veda* differ a lot. In *Sãma Veda* seven *swars* (sound) are used.

The songs to be sung in a village are known as *Uhagãna* and the songs to be sung in forests are known as *Uhyagãna*.

The seven *swars*, according to the First Chapter of *Sãmavidhãna Brãhman*, are *Krushta, Prathma, Dwitiya, Tritiya, Chaturth, Mandra* and *Atiswãra*. These seven *swars* satisfy the hunger of gods, human, animals, birds, *gandharvas*, *apsarãs*, demons and immovable things.

The Ten Nights Festival known as ***Dashrãtra*** is the most important festival of the followers of *Sãma Veda*. It is concluded with '*Gawãmayana*'. There are three parts in *Sãma Gãna* Divison:

- The *Sãma* in which only *richãs* are sung is called ***'Ãbi sangyaka'***.
- The *Sãma* in which only the *stobha* are sung is called ***'Lesha sangyaka'***.
- The singing of complete *stobha* is called ***'Chhanna sangyaka'***.

While those in which '*hãu*', '*auhowã*' and '*ida*' like syllables (other than the *ric* syllables) are used are called '*Stobha*'. Some of them are — *dãnenãdãnam, akrodhena krodham, shradhayãshradhãm* and *satyenãnritam*.

The scattered material on music was collected, contemplated upon and given a definite and systematic shape in *Sāma Veda*. Hence, it is unanimously accepted when Bharat Muni said that music takes its birth from *Sāma Veda*: ***Sāmabhyo geetameva cha.***

It is said by Shārangadeva in *Sangeet Ratnākar* that Brahmā collected songs in the *Sāma Veda*: ***Sāmavedādidam geetam sanjagrāha pitāmahah.***

In the *Gitā* (10:22), Lord Shri Krishna stamped the authenticity by claiming: ***Vedānāma Sāmavedoasmi*** (Among the Vedas, I'm *Sāma Veda*).

In one sense, *Sāma Veda* represents all the Vedas and is in itself a complete Veda as it contains the poetic *mantras* of *Rig Veda*; the prosaic *mantras* of *Yajur Veda,* and in addition to them it has lyrical songs. That is one reason why *Sāma Veda* as so important and why its songs are sung with devotion and dedication. The real objective behind *Sāma Veda* is to fulfil wishes and desires.

4. Atharva Veda

The other three Vedas are famous as *Vedatrai.* These three Vedas have been named on the basis of the integral qualities of the *mantras* as *Ric, Yajuh* and *Sāma*. But *Atharva Veda* is different. It has many different names: *Atharva Veda, Atharvāngiroveda, Atharvāngiras, Brahmaveda, Bhishagveda* and *Kshatraveda.*

Atharva Veda is last in the series of the *Veda Samhitās*. Some people think and claim that it is not very ancient but this Veda is as ancient as the other three because this Veda too was edited by Ved Vyās and taught by him.

The fact is that, to begin with, there was a single collection of *mantras* and the collection continued to grow. Ultimately Ved Vyās had a great collection of other *mantras* envisioned by various *rishis*. He had no other way but to divide them into three groups so that people could memorise, learn, understand and teach them separately.

The *mantras* that Ved Vyas got later and the knowledge that he gathered about other *rishis* were compiled in the fourth Veda. So, no one can claim that the *mantras* of this Veda were seen by *rishis* after the other collections were ready. It proves only one thing that the *mantras* of *Atharva Veda* were made known to Ved Vyās when he had already compiled the *Veda-trai*. When the *rishis* who had these *mantras* came to know about the fresh compilation being done, they brought their collection to him.

Since neither the Vedas nor the *mantras* are ever deluded and lost or forgotten or unavailable, *mantras* were recovered by the later *rishis*, so all the other mantras found place in the fourth Veda.

The present day race towards the scriptures, the Vedas and the *rishis* indicates that a fresh generation of 'NEW

RISHIS' is at hand and they will surely recover the lost *mantras* and numerous lost scriptures. It is just a matter of some patience.

It is not our hypothesis that is important. It is the ancient writing that must be seen in its true form and without prejudice. The conditions were different during the period of slavery but at present Indians are not slaves. They can read what is written and also that which has not been written or said for they are the descendents of those *rishis* who wrote these books. The slavery of one thousand years has taken a heavy toll but the freedom of last sixty years has returned back a major part of the knowledge of the ancient past and has also given birth to a great deal of the new knowledge of the country, world, Space and the Universe. We now know what exactly our forefathers meant when they worshipped Brahmã and tried their best to achieve Oneness for *moksha* or salvation.

Before coming to any conclusion, let us read about the the story of *Atharva* and *Angirãs* as given in *Gopatha Brahman*:

During the time immemorial, after the great delude, it was time to start the creation again. Swayambhu Brahmã was in deep penance meditating over the new creation when his sperm was discharged in water surrounded by sands in an oasis. The *maharshi* named **Bhrigu** was born out of it. He was passionately in search of Brahmā. He heard a sound from the sky:

Atharvā anametā swewā psawanwichchha

— *Gopatha Brahman* (1:4)

(O Atharva! Search that invisible Brahmā in that water.)

From then on **Bhrigu** became **Atharva.**

Once again there was another discharge of fluids from Brahmā in the sandy water. This time it was very different. It was the discharge of sweat-like fluid from each part of Brahmā. Another maharshi named **Angirā** was born out of it. Both Bhrigu and Angirā were inspired by Brahma to go for penance. Two elements found in water are these two, Bhrigu and Angirā, called Hydrogen and Oxygen.

It was the effect of their great and prolonged penance that twenty Atharvas and Angirās were born who envisioned two *mantras* each. During their penance, Brahmā envisioned *mantras* through them. Those *mantras* were kept separate and when they were compiled, they became the *Atharvāngirasa Veda* or the *Atharva Veda.* Since the number of *rishi* was 20, so this Veda was also divided in 20 *kāndas* (chapters).

The *Atharva Veda* is the combined knowledge of the *Atharvas* and *Angirās. Atharvas* represent peaceful and healthy deeds and *Angirās* represent extreme deeds. The *Atharva Veda*

Samhitā (*Shaunak Shākhā*) has 20 *kāndas*, 730 *suktas*, 36 *prapāthakas* and 5987 *mantras*. Starting with four *mantras*, one *mantra* has been added to each subsequent *kāndas* up to 5th and suddenly the number of *suktas* rises up to 142 in the 6th *kānda*. About one-sixth of its hymns are common with the *Rig Veda*. Most of the verses are metrical, but some sections are in prose.

The *Atharva Veda* is preserved and available in two branches (recensions): the *Paippalāda* and *Shaunaka*. The *Paippalāda* version is longer than the *Shaunaka* one. Its first part consists chiefly of spells and incantations, concerned with protection against demons and disaster, spells for the healing of diseases, and for long life. The second part of the text contains speculative and philosophical hymns.

The following constitute the subject matter of *Atharva Veda*.

Brahman

Brahman is the main subject dealt in it which is not available in other *Samhitās*. That is the reason why *Atharva Veda* is called *Brahmaveda* also. It answers a number of inquisitive questions such as:

What is *Brahman*? What is His form? Where and how can we find Him? Is He one or many? What is His relationship with gods and goddesses?

Besides these questions, *Atharva Veda* also shows the relationship between God, living beings and Nature.

Creation

Atharva Veda says that the creation of living beings started in water. God placed seeds (cells) in water which took the form of an egg, known as *Hiranyagarbh*. Life came on the earth from there on.

Treatment of Diseases

The treatment of different diseases is scattered throughout *Atharva Veda*. Most of the treatments are in the form of *mantras* and prayers; and the names of medicines are given in *Bhaisajya Suktas*. A detailed account of treatment of mental diseases is also given. Among other treatments, the treatment through water and the rays of sun are given prominence.

Politics and Governance

Atharva Veda deals with the rights and duties of both the kings and the citizens. The selection of a king, the ceremony when the selected king is placed on the throne, the type of governance, creation of different departments and committees, justice and punishment, soldiers, army, forms of war, enemies, attacks and ways to win a battle are discussed and explained in detail.

Health and Long Life

A healthy life is a boon and a long life is an achievement. This Veda has suggestions and *mantras* for both these aspects of life. It is needless to state that health and long life are the wish of every man and woman.

One thing is certain that there were diseases even during that primitive period and man had started making efforts to get rid of them. Other than the medicines, the offering of prayers, wearing stones and jewels, and binding the wrist veins with thread (*rakshā-sutra*) were commonly in practice as advocated in *Atharva Veda.*

Peaceful and Healthy Deeds

The *rishis* prayed and asked the people to pray and lead a clean and pure life. Most of the prayers are aimed at suggesting ways and means to avoid and to be free from loss, accidents, pain, nightmares by doing good deeds and by praying to God. There are many *suktas* of this kind in the *Atharva Veda.*

Destructive Deeds

There are many ways and prayers suggested to destroy the demons and the enemies. These are known as *Abhichāra Karma* which include *mantras* like *Vashikaran* (mesmerism), *Mārak* (killing), *Mohini* (enchanting) and *Uchchātan* (separation and uprooting).

Introspection and Expiation

One must meditate and look at one's deeds and misdeeds so that he can remain free from evil deeds and perform only wholesome ones. When one does something wrong, one must punish oneself so that such wrong deeds are not repeated in the future. One must go for atonement and expiation to be free from the sins committed in such ways. *Prayers are a way to purge the heart and mind.*

Compassion

Compassion for other living beings is a great quality. One must work and pray for love, affection and cooperation among the family members, in society and in the best of the interests of the country.

Four Objects of Man's Pursuit

In short, it can be concluded that all the four common and constant pursuits of man: *Dharma* (Religion), *Artha* (Income), *Kāma* (Work and Sex) and *Moksha* (Salvation) have been discussed in *Atharva Veda* for a better, peaceful and happy life. Aesthetic sense, perfect diction, beauty of language, figures of speech and metres are at their respective best in this Veda. Moreover, it is a store of general knowledge, politics, economics, theology and sociology.

Modern man must bow down to the *rishis* particularly to their fertile and mature disposition, and deep and great thinking, and to the fact that they thought about each malady in personal, social and political life and suggested ways to minimise them or to get rid of them completely.

The *rishis* were simply great. The Vedas that they compiled are the greatest storehouse of human knowledge. Every known branch of knowledge is an offshoot of Vedas.

Shãkhãs of Vedas

There are different *shãkhãs* (branches) of each Veda. There are total 1131 *shãkhãs* of the four Vedas.

Rig Veda

It is said that *Rig Veda* has 21 branches but only one is available — *Shãkala Shãkhã*. Besides this, *Vãshkala Shãkhã*, *Ãshwãlãyana Shãkhã*, *Shãnkhãyana Shãkhã* and *Mãndukãyana Shãkhã* are also under there.

Yajur Veda

There are total 101 branches of *Yajur Veda*. *Yajur Veda Mantra Samhita* is divided in two parts:

- *Shukla Yajur Veda*
- *Krishna Yajur Veda*

It is claimed that *Shukla Yajur Veda* had 15 branches and *Krishna Yajur Veda* had 86 branches making the total 101 branches.

Shukla Yajur Veda

Out of the 15 branches only 2 branches are available.

1. *Kãnva*
2. *Mãdhyãndin*

Krishna Yajur Veda

The following are the 5 branches of *Krishna Yajur Veda* which are available.

1. *Taitteriya*
2. *Maitrãyini*
3. *Katha*
4. *Kãpisthal*
5. *Shwetãswar*

Sãma Veda

1000 branches of *Sãma Veda* are mentioned but only 3 are available.

1. *Kauthumi* (complete)
2. *Jaiminiyã* (complete)
3. *Rãnãyaniyã* (partly)

Atharva Veda

Out of the 9 branches of *Atharva Veda*, only 2 are found.

1. *Paippalādi*
2. *Shaunkiyā*

The other 7 unavailable branches are: *Tauda, Mauda, Jājala, Jalada, Brahmavada, Devadarsha* and *Chāranavaida.*

Brahman Granthas

How the *mantras* should be used and recited, is dealt in detail in the *Brahman Granthas*. The *Brahman Granthas* are wonderful creations. Some people claim that only the *mantra Samhitās* and the *Brahman Granthas* constitute the complete Veda. It seems to be an exaggeration, for other treatises have so much to give that in absence of those great books, the meaning of the *mantras* cannot be understood and the human knowledge will remain incomplete forever.

Just like the *shākhās*, the *Brahman Granthas* are also 1,131 in number. But only the following are available:

- **The *Brahman Granthas* of *Rig Veda***
  1. *Aitareya Brahman*
  2. *Shākhāyan Brahman* or *Kaushitaki Brahman*
- **The *Brahman Granthas* of *Shukla Yajur Veda***
  1. *Shatpatha Brahman* (*Kānva Shākhā*)
  2. *Shatpatha Brahman* (*Mādhyāndin Shākhā*)

Shatpatha Brahman

The best and biggest *Brahman Grantha* is *Shukla Yajur Veda's Shatpatha Brahman.* It has presented its subject matter in a complete and comprehensive way. With a bit of changes in the sequence of the chapters, the *Shatpatha Brahmans* of both the *shākhās* (*kānva* and *mādhyandin*) are the same.

Shatpatha Brahman has 14 ***kānds***, 438 ***brahman***, and 7,624 ***kandikās*** which are arranged in 100 chapters. Because of the 100 chapters, it is called *Shatpatha*: ***shatam panthāno yasya tatchchhatapatham.***

This book meticulously describes different forms of *yajnas* and all related and relevant *Anushthāns* (rituals). Such things are not available in other *Brahman Granthas.*

It lays great stress on *Agnihotra* and claims that an *Agnihotri* never perishes even after death.

Agni (fire) is a boat for an *Agnihotri* to take him to heaven: ***naurah wā yeshā swargyā yadi Agnihotram.***

Shatpatha declares *yajna* to be the most important task in life: ***yagyo wai shreshtam karmam.***

It presents all the related rituals of a *yajna* in minute detail.

- **The *Brahman Granthas* of *Krishna Yajur Veda***
    1. *Tāitteriya Brahman*
    2. *Madhyavarti Brahman*

- The *Brahman Granthas* of *Sãma Veda*
  1. *Tãndya* (*Panchvinsh*) *Brahman*
  2. *Shadvinsh Brahman*
  3. *Sãmvidhãn Brahman*
  4. *Ãrsheya Brahman*
  5. *Mantra Brahman*
  6. *Daivatãdhyãya Brahman*
  7. *Bansh Brahman*
  8. *Samhitopanishad Brahman*
  9. *Jaiminiya Brahman*
  10. *Jaiminiya-Upanishad Brahman*

Tãndya (Panchvinsh) Brahman

The name *Tãndya Brahman* was given to it because it has 25 chapters, and because it is the largest among all the *Brahman Granthas*, it is called *Mahã Brahman*. It deals with *Audagãtra Karma*. In order to explain and illustrate its main theme, this *Brahman Grantha* takes the help of tales and anecdotes; for example *Veengk Sãma Gãna* (14:6:10) tells the story of Chyavan *rishi*. It has described how old Chyavan *rishi* was metamorphosed into a young and healthy man.

There is a famous story about *Sãma-Vatsa* in *Tãndya Brahman* (14:6:6):

There were two famous Kãnva *rishis*. They were Vatsa and Medhãtithi. Once hot debate began between the two, in which Medhãtithi challenged the very *Brahmanatva* of Vatsa by calling him a *shudra* (non-Brahmin). It was an open humiliation and Vatsa was not willing to accept it. The debate grew and at last it was decided to test the *Brahmanatva* of Vatsa. Vatsa was ready for that. Both Vatsa and Medhãtithi recited their own creations of *Sãma mantras* namely '*Vatsa Sãma*' and '*Medhatithi Sãma*'. Then they came to *Agni*. Vatsa repeated his *Vatsa Sãma* and entered the fire but the fire did not touch him. Thus the *Brahmanatva* of Vatsa was proved and established.

Shadvinsh Brahman

Shadvinsh Brahman is divided into 6 chapters but it is usually taken as the 26th chapter of the above discussed *Tãndya Brahman*. It deals with the wonderful and unbelievable incidents that usually occur in our life basically with *Smãrta Yãga* like lightning falling on a house, tussle with officers, sudden deaths of horses and elephants, earthquakes, blood oozing out from trees and the birth of handicapped children etc. The descriptions of gods as *chakrapãnaye, dandapãnaye* or *shoolpãnaye* form the basis of construction of the idols of gods in modern times sculptured on these patterns with human body and some weapons in their hands.

Sãmvidhãn Brahman

Sãmvidhãn Brahman is divided into 3 chapters in which it is imagined and explained that the Almighty gave *Sãma* as food to satiate the hunger of man. The hunger was satiated with only the seven notes of the *Sãma Gãna*. But the times changed and man became a different creature.

Ãrsheya Brahman

Ãrsheya Brahman is divided into 6 chapters and deals with the life and achievements of the *rishis* related to *Sãma Gãna* only. In fact, *Ãrsheya* is the name of the *Brahman* who gave the names of *Mantradrashtã rishis* as the names of the *Sãmas*.

The chapter *Devtãdhyãya Brahman* gives the names of the gods of *Sãma* on the basis of *Nidhana*.

- **The *Brahman Grantha* of *Atharva Veda***

1. *Gopatha Brahman*

Only one *Brahman Grantha* of *Atharva Veda* is available. The discourse delivered by Maharshi Gopatha is known as the *Gopatha Brahman*. It is divided into two parts:

2. *Purva Gopatha*
3. *Uttara Gopatha*

In the former, there are 5 *Prapãthakas* and 135 *Kandikãs* and in the latter, there are 6 *Prapãthakas* and 123 *Kandikãs*.

Gopatha Brahman

It is said that once *Gopatha Brahman* had 100 *Prapāthakas* but today only 11 *Prapāthakas* are found. It is mentioned in its 49th Appendix named *Charanvyuha.*

Gopatha Brahman opens with the process of creation. After the story of the birth of the two *rishis*, it switches over to *Aum* and the *Tri* (three is needed for balance). It proceeds to discuss the importance of *Aum* which is the cause and force behind the creation. Then it discusses the fruits of the recitations of *Aum* and answers 36 questions regarding *Aum* (1:1:16-30).

It establishes the rule that *Aum* should be pronounced before the recitation of every *mantra* (1:1:28). It ends with detailed analysis of the *Gāyatri Mantra.*

For the first time in a *Brahman Grantha*, the *Kārikās* of Grammar are mentioned (1:1:25-27).

The second *Prapāthaka* deals with celibacy, admonishes from sitting on a higher pedestal and inflicting injury to others. It lays emphasis that one must maintain celibacy for 48 years if one wishes to learn the Vedas. It concludes with the role of *ritwiks* in a *yajna.*

Gopatha Brahman has given the meaning and etymology of many words including *Varun*. The last three *Prapāthakas* are dedicated to the knowledge of *Brahman* and how one can become a *Brahman.*

The second part is mostly confined to *yajnas* and stories related to them.

Āranyakas

Āranyakas are associated with and named after the *shākhās* (branches) of Vedas.

Rig Veda

1. *Aitareya Āranyaka* belongs to the *Shākala Shākhā.*
2. *Kaushitaki Āranyaka* is associated both with the *Kaushitaki* and *Shānkhyāyana Shākhā* of *Rig Veda.*

Krishna Yajur Veda

1. *Taitteriya Āranyaka* belongs to *Krishna Yajur Veda's* branch of the same name.
2. *Katha Āranyaka* is associated with *Katha* and *Charaka Shākhā.*
3. *Maittrāyaniya Āranyaka* belongs to *Maittrāyaniya* branch.

Sāma Veda

1. *Tālavākara Āranyaka* belongs to the *Jaiminiya Shākhā.*

Atharva Veda

1. Earlier there were *Āranyakas* of *Atharva Veda* but now *Atharva Veda* has no surviving *Āranyaka.*

Āranyakas discuss philosophy and sacrifice, and the philosophy behind the sacrifices. They are a philosophical and mystical interpretation of the themes of the *mantras*. That is the reason why Durgāchārya wrote in his commentary on *Niruktas* that the *Āranyakas* are *Rahasya Brahmans* which lay ample stress on 'One Absolute Reality'.

They differ from both *Brahmans* and *Upanishads.* While the *Brahmans* are primarily concerned with the proper performance of *yajnas*, rituals and rites, the *Upanishads* are more concerned with knowing the *Brahman*. In the end, *Āranyakas* are closer to *Upanishads* and bear almost the same names which may mislead people into thinking that they are the same books.

In *Āranyakas,* the themes of the Vedas are directly and individually conveyed to the pupil by the teachers. They constitute a secret or hidden teaching but not a forbidden one. Details of three *Āranyakas* are given below:

Aitareya Āranyaka

It contains five chapters. Each of them is considered to be a full *Āranyaka*.

The **first** chapter of the *Āranyaka* deals with *Mahābhārata* both in its worldly and divine forms.

The **second** chapter is divided into six parts. They are all treated as proper chapters and not the sub-chapters. Their first chapter deals with *Prāna-Vidyā* which is also *Prāna-Vāyu* and constitutes the life-breath or life-element in a living being. The Vedas, Vedic *mantras* and all Vedic declarations have been accepted as living body, hence they all possess that *Prāna-Vāyu*. The *rishis* have been compared to *Prāna-Tatwa* on different grounds:

- **Vishwāmitra** for the word *vishwa* (Universe) is the object of the experience of *Prāna-Deva*.
- **Vāmadeva** for the word *vāma* is respectable and worthy enough to be worshipped.
- **Atri** for having *trāyate* in his name which is synonymous to protector.
- **Bhāradwāja** for having *bhāra* (support) and *wāja* (the mortal body) as he supports the mortal body.
- **Brahmarishi Vashishtha** for *vas* (body) and *istha* (dwelling) as he dwells in this body in the form of *Prana*.

The rest of the chapters constitute the famous *Āranyaka Upanishad*.

The **third** chapter is known as *Samhitopanishad.*

The **fourth** chapter is known as *Mahānāmni Mantras.*

The **fifth** and the last chapter is famous as *Mādhyandin Yajna.*

Taitteriya Āranyaka

It has ten chapters which deal with the following:

Chapters and Contents

1	*Surya Namaskār*
2	Five *Mahā Yajnas*
3	*Homas* and *Yajnas*
4	*Mantras* that can avert destructions
5	General treatises on *Yajnas*
6	*Pitri-Medhā Mantra* recited at the pyre
7 to 9	*Taitteriya Upanishad*
10	*Mahā Nārāyana Upanishad*

Kaushitaki Āranyaka

It has fifteen chapters which deal with the following:

Chapters and Contents

1	*Mahābhārata*
2	*Mahābhārata*
3 to 6	*Kaushitaki Upanishad*
7 & 8	*Samhitopanishad*

9 Discussion of the greatness of *Prāna*

10 *Agnihotra* Ritual

11 Rituals for warding off death and sickness

12 Happy results of Prayers

13 *Shravana, Manana, Nidhidhyāsana*

14 I'm *Brahman*

15 Geneology from *Brahmā* to *Guna-Shānkhyāyana*

Upanishads

The *Upanishads* are treated as the basic foundation of the teachings of the Vedas given by the *rishis* to the *tapaswis* and their disciples in the *aranyās* (forests) where the disciples would sit near the *rishis* to get at the bottom of the eternal truth. Such treatises are called *Upanishads* whose literal meaning is 'sitting down by the side of'.

It is the real representative of the *Guru-Shishya-Paramparā* (teacher and disciple tradition). They give the *Brahman-jnāna* to their disciples. They discuss philosophy, meditation, nature and form of God. They are the mystic and spiritual contemplations of Vedas. They form the part of *Vedānta*, the conclusion of Vedas which is evident from *Brahma-Sutra* by Ved Vyās. Some people foolishly think that *Vedānta* is the end or culmination of Vedas while it is the conclusion from where begins the search for the *Brahman:* ***athāto Brahman jigyāsā***. *Upanishads* are purely spiritual thinking.

The *Upanishads* are also said to be 1131 in number but only 275 are found. Out of those 275 *Upanishads*, 108 are famous and accepted as authentic while 11 out of these 108 are very important.

Many *achāryās*, including Shankarāchārya, have written *Bhashya* on them.

The 11 most important *Upanishads* are:

1. *Isha*	2. *Kena*	3. *Katha*
4. *Mundak*	5. *Māndukya*	6. *Prashna*
7. *Aitareya*	8. *Taitteriya*	9. *Chhāndogya*
10. *Brihadaranyaka*	11. *Shwetāswar*	

1. Ishāvāsyopanishad

Mantras	Subject
1-2	To remember the Absolute and work with detachment
3	Those who go against it suffer immensely
4-5	The form of the Absolute *Brahman*
6-8	The position of those who know the Absolute *Brahman*
9-11	The elements of worshipping *Vidyā* and *Avidyā*
12-14	The elements of worshipping *Sambhuti* and *Asambhuti*

15-16	What to pray during the last phase
17	What to pray at the time of death
18	Prayer to Agni while going to the other world

2. Kenopanishad

Kena and *Chhāndogya*, the famous *Upanishads* of *Sāma Veda*, discuss and analyse different themes. The last three chapters of *Chhāndogya Upanishad* deal with Spiritual Science.

Chapter/Mantras	**Subject**
1/1-8	What inspires the sense organs? Symbolic description of the Absolute God in the form of energy and energy-giver
2/1-5	*Brahman-jnāna,* feelings, to know *Brahman-tatwa*
3/1-12	The ego in *Devatās*, appearance of *Yaksha*, ego of Fire, Air and Indra subdued by *Yaksha*, Umādevi answers Indra
4/1-9	Umādevi teaches *Brahman-tatwa* with different examples, the ways and results of worshipping the Absolute *Brahman*

3. Kathopanishad

Kathopanishad is divided in two chapters and each chapter has three *Vallis*.

Chapter/Valli/ Mantras	Subject
1/1/1-9	Yajna by Maharshi Uddālaka, Nachiketā given to Yama, he reaches Yamaloka; receives three blessings from Yama
1/1/10-22	First blessing — happiness to father, second blessing — the secret of *Agni*, and the third blessing — revelation of the self; first two given, Yama describes difficulties in the third
1/1/23-29	Yama promises to give a lot if the third question is withdrawn, Nachiketā remains adamant
1/2/1-13	Yama teaches *Brahman-vidyā*, praises those who know this science, the greatness of *Brahman*
1/2/14-25	As an answer Yama teaches *Aum*, describes Self and the Absolute, why people fail to get united with Him
1/3/1-9	The relation between living beings and *Brahman*, prayer is the best way, comparison of ignorant and wise
1/3/10-17	To control the senses from going astray; importance of knowing and ways to know Him, warnings and results

2/1/1-15	Senses are hindrances in knowing Him, to be free from vices, his description as Aditi, Agni and the Sun, the cycle of birth, *Brahman* is as big as the thumb
2/2/1-15	Freedom from suffering and salvation, oneness and perfection everywhere, form of Brahman, how to get bliss and beatitude, *Brahman* as omnipresent light
2/3/1-9	Banyan tree, getting Nectar, He rules everywhere, Self is beyond perception by senses
2/3/10-18	Yoga, faith, detached and without doubt, life after death, salvation, Nachiketā gets united

4. Prashnopanishad

Questions/Mantras	Subject
1/1-8	Kabandhi asks about birth, Pippalāda answers — God created Universe by uniting *Prāna* and *Rayi*
1/9	Worshipping with *Prāna* and *Rayi*, *Surya* in his form within month/day, prohibition of sex during the day, grains are god, *Prajāpati brata*, truthfulness and a life without vices leads to Heaven, *Brahmaloka*

2/1-13	Bhãrgava asks about gods who possess and lighten body, greatness of *Prãna* and its eulogy
3/1-12	Aswalãyana's 6 questions regarding *Prãna*, creation by Him, *Prãna-vãyu* explained, changing body by *prãna*, worldly and ethereal outcome of this knowledge
4/1-11	Gãrya's 5 questions regarding living being and God, senses during sleep, ever awakened 5 *Prãnas*, sleep and state of dream, peace by union
5/1-7	Satyakãm's question about *Aum*, *Aum* is God, worshipping *Aum* is to get all heavens
6/1	Sukeshã's question about man with 16 qualities, such one is the Creator, element of perfect man, salvation

5. Mundakopanishad

Chapter	Subject
1/part 1	*Parã-Aparã-Vidyã*, the sequence of creation
1/part 2	Its form and results, types of flame, attachments and detachment, need of guru, analytical teaching
2/part 1	Creation by fire and return to fire, infinite form of *Brahman*, creation of rivers and emotions etc

2/part 2	Description of '*Guhāchar*' God, how to hit the target, meditation on self-like God, self-illuminated, omnipresent
3/part 1	Metaphor of birds, egolessness, penance and celibacy are the ways, purity gives power, success for enlightened
3/part 2	Weaknesses and failure, intense desire succeeds, *Brahman-vidyā* and ways of teaching, persons to be taught

6. Māndukyopanishad

Mantras	Subject
1	Past, present and future are forms of *Aum, Omkār*
2	Four steps of the union of *Brahman* and *Aum, Omkār*
3	First step *Vaishwānar* described
4	Second step *Hiranyagarbh Taijas* described
5	Third step blissful *Prāgya* described
6	Why is *Brahman* Omniscient and God of all
7	Fourth step formless *Brahman* without qualities described
8	Three syllables of *Pranava Aum*

9	First syllable with *Vaiswānar* associated
10	Second syllable with *Taijas* associated
11	Third syllable with *Prāgya* associated
12	Knowing *Brahman* without syllable as fourth step

7. Aitareya Upanishad

Chapter	Subject
1/part 1	Desire to create, creation of all Universe, Prajāpati and gods
1/part 2	Prayer for grain by senses and their gods, creation of cows, horses and man, gods enter man at their places, share their thirst and hunger from the shares of gods
1/part 3	Grains created, run away, man fails to catch them with senses, caught grains through *Apāna-Vāyu*, God enters body through *Vidriti* door, ecstasy of man at creation, God takes the name Indra
2	First embryo in mother's womb and care by her, birth, relation with parents and duties, responsibility of a son, death and rebirth, third life, Vāmadeva enlightened in womb

3	*Rishis* think over God and beings, existence of God established, *rishis* declare Him to be the Creator and Protector, becoming immortal after death, in Heaven

8. Taitteriya Upanishad

Taitteriya Upanishad is divided into three Vallis known as ***Shikshā Valli***, ***Brahmānand Valli*** and ***Bhrigu Valli***, and the *mantras* have been replaced by '**Anuwāka**'.

Anuwāka	Subject
1-12	***Shikshā Valli*** — Prayer by the names of gods and Vāyu, rules of pronunciation of *mantras*, growth and development of different things and part, Omkār prayer, character of teachers/disciples, power of emotion, to be a householder
1-9	***Brahmānand Valli*** — Knowing God living in self, *Annamaya*, *Prānamaya*, *Manomaya* body and Self described, blissful *Brahman*, what knower gets
1-10	***Bhrigu Valli*** — Everything is *Brahman*, *Grain-Brahman*, *Prāna-Brahman*, Mind-*Brahman*, Being-*Brahman* and blissful God is *Brahman*, increase production, stop wastages, *Brahman* is Perfect

9. Shwetãswaropanishad

Chapters/Mantras	Subject
1/1-8	Causes behind creation, time, nature, destiny, revelation through meditation, cycle of Universe as a river, imprisonment of soul in body and liberation
1/9-16	Form of Being, nature, God, Omkãr, revelation, God within
2	Prayer, meditation, *pranãyãma*, *siddhi*, health
2	Yoga, freedom from all ties, *Antaryãmi Brahman*
3/1-17	Knowledge and Nectar, cycle, omnipresence, prayer to Omniscient, freedom from suffering, thumb-like God
3/18-21	Imperceptible within nine doors, without organs does all, God is infinite, revealing experience
4/1-11	Prayer for pure mind, tied ignorant, illusion and the Master, peace by knowing
4/12-22	Offerings, detailed description of absolutely subtle *Brahman*, prayer for salvation
5/1-7	Secrets of self-illuminating God, changes by mixing qualities with created beings, birth in many forms

5/8-14	Birth as man, growth of body, causes behind cycle, ways to be free from the cycle of birth and death
6/1-13	Creation by God only, ways of worship, eulogy, immense power of the Creator, salvation to knower
6/14-23	Illumination from His Light only, shelter of Lord, no salvation without Him, success of devotees

Here is a list of 108 *Upanishads* which are famous and accepted as authentic:

The Upanishads of Rig Veda

1. *Aitareya Upanishad*
2. *Akshamālik Upanishad*
3. *Ātmabodha Upanishad*
4. *Bhavrichā Upanishad*
5. *Kaushitaki Upanishad*
6. *Mudagala Upanishad*
7. *Nāda Upanishad*
8. *Nirvāna Upanishad*
9. *Saubhāgyalakshmi Upanishad*
10. *Tripura Upanishad*

The Upanishads of Shukla Yajur Veda

1. *Ādhyātma Upanishad*
2. *Advaiyatārak Upanishad*
3. *Bhikshu Upanishad*
4. *Brihadākāranyaka Upanishad*
5. *Hamsā Upanishad*
6. *Ishāvasya Upanishad*
7. *Jabālā Upanishad*
8. *Mandalbrāhman Upanishad*
9. *Māntrika Upanishad*
10. *Muktika Upanishad*
11. *Nirālambā Upanishad*
12. *Paingalā Upanishad*
13. *Paramahamsā Upanishad*
14. *Satyāyani Upanishad*
15. *Subālā Upanishad*
16. *Tārāsarā Upanishad*
17. *Trishkhibrāhman Upanishad*
18. *Turiyātita Upanishad*
19. *Yāgyavalkya Upanishad*

Out of these 19 *Upanishads* of *Shukla Yajur Veda,* two are important. They are ***Brihadaranyaka Upanishad*** and ***Ishāvāsyopanishad.***

In the *Mādhyandin Āranyaka*, the ***Brihadaranyaka Upanishad*** constitutes the 14th chapter while in *Kānva* branch it is the 17th.

Most of the *Brahman Granthas* contain their *Upanishads* at the end but in the case of *Shukla Yajur Veda's* ***Shatpatha Brahman*** it is entirely different.

The discourse has been delivered by *Yāgyavalkya*. Because of great similarities as both are related to mysticism, *Āranyak* and *Upanishads* are often treated as one yet they are different books for the subtle variations in the subject matter and approach and treatment.

The main subject matter of the *Āranyakas* is the worshipping of 'Life Element' whereas *Upanishads* deal mostly with the 'Spiritual Elements' in *yajna* and rituals. For that basic philosophy the *Upanishads* are given preference over many other categories of treatises.

The Upanishads of Krishna Yajur Veda

1. *Akshi Upanishad*
2. *Amritabindu Upanishad*
3. *Amrita Nād Upanishad*
4. *Avadhuta Upanishad*
5. *Brahma Upanishad*
6. *Brahma Vidyā Upanishad*

7. *Dakshinãmurti Upanishad*
8. *Dhyãnabindu Upanishad*
9. *Ekãkshar Upanishad*
10. *Garbha Upanishad*
11. *Kaivalya Upanishad*
12. *Kãlagnirudra Upanishad*
13. *Kalisantaran Upanishad*
14. *Karopnishad*
15. *Kathopnishad*
16. *Kshurikopnishad*
17. *Nãrãyanopanishad*
18. *Panchbrahma Upanishad*
19. *Prãnagnihotra Upanishad*
20. *Rudrahridya Upanishad*
21. *Saraswatirahasya Upanishad*
22. *Sarvãsar Upanishad*
23. *Sharirakopanishad*
24. *Skanda Upanishad*
25. *Shukarahasya Upanishad*
26. *Shwetãswar Upanishad*
27. *Taittiriya Upanishad*
28. *Tejobindu Upanishad*

29. *Vārāhopanishad*
30. *Yogakundalini Upanishad*
31. *Yoga Shikshā Upanishad*
32. *Yogatatva Upanishad*

The Upanishads of Sāma Veda

1. *Āruni Upanishad*
2. *Avyakta Upanishad*
3. *Chhandogya Upanishad*
4. *Darshan Upanishad*
5. *Jabālādarshan Upanishad*
6. *Jabāli Upanishad*
7. *Kena Upanishad*
8. *Kundika Upanishad*
9. *Mahātsanyās Upanishad*
10. *Maitreyi Upanishad*
11. *Maitrāyani Upanishad*
12. *Rudrākshajabālā Upanishad*
13. *Sāvitri Upanishad*
14. *Vajrasuchikā Upanishad*
15. *Vāsudeva Upanishad*
16. *Chudāmani Upanishad*

The Upanishads of Atharva Veda

1. *Annapurnā Upanishad*
2. *Atharvashira Upanishad*
3. *Atharvashikha Upanishad*
4. *Ātmopanishad*
5. *Bhāvnopanishad*
6. *Bhasmopanishad*
7. *Brihatjabālopnishad*
8. *Devi Upanishad*
9. *Dattaitreya Upanishad*
10. *Ganapati Upanishad*
11. *Garydopanishad*
12. *Gopālatapāni Upanishad*
13. *Hayagrivopnishad*
14. *Krishna Upanishad*
15. *Mahānārāyana Upanishad*
16. *Mahāvākya Upanishad*
17. *Māndukya Upanishad*
18. *Mundakopanishad*
19. *Nāradparivrājaka Upanishad*
20. *Narsimhatapāni Upanishad*
21. *Pārabrahma Upanishad*

22. *Paramhamsaparivrājaka Upanishad*
23. *Pasupata Upanishad*
24. *Prasnopanishad*
25. *Ramarahasya Upanishad*
26. *Sita Upanishad*
27. *Rāmaatapāni Upanishad*
28. *Shāndilya Upanishad*
29. *Sarbhā Upanishad*
30. *Surya Upanishad*
31. *Tripurtapāni Upanishad*

Sutra Granthas in Vedas

In the Vedas, the *Sutra shakha* (branch) has *sutras* of three different varieties known as:

a. ***Shroutsutra***
b. ***Grihyasutra***
c. ***Dharmasutra***

There are two types of *Shroutsutras*:

- ***Drāhyāyana***
- ***Lātyāyan***

In the same way, two types of *Grihyasutras* are there:

- ***Khādir***
- ***Govil***

The **North Indians** who study and sing *Sāma Veda*, follow *Lātyāyan Shroutsutra* and *Govil Grihyasutra.*

The **South Indians** follow *Drāhyāyana Shroutsutra* and *Khādir Grihyasutra.*

There is another type of *sutra* known as *Sulvasutra* which may be a part of another *sutra*. It is said that the *Sulvasutras* dealt with physics but since they are not available hence physics in the Vedas is not known. A few *Sulvasutras* are, however, available. All the Vedas have their different *sutras.* But unfortunately most of them are not available. They were destroyed during different battles and calamities.

In the *Shroutsutras* the rites and rituals, the *karmakānd* of the *mantras* from the *Samhitās* have been explained and elucidated.

In the *Dharmasutras,* the religious rituals have been described.

The *Sutra Granthas* in Vedas are as follows:

The Sutras of Rig Veda

1. *Āswalāyan Shroutsutra*
2. *Shānkhāyan Shroutsutra*
3. *Āswalāyan Grihyasutra*
4. *Shānkhāyan Grihyasutra*
5. *Vashishtha Dharmasutra*

The Sutras of Shukla Yajur Veda

1. *Kātyāyan Shroutsutra*
2. *Pāraskar Shroutsutra*
3. *Pāraskar Grihyasutra*
4. *Kātyāyan Dharmasutra*
5. *Vishnu Dharmasutra*

Among the *Shroutsutras* of *Shukla Yajur Veda* perhaps only the *Kātyāyan Shroutsutra* is available in its complete form. It holds an important position among the *Shroutsutras.* It is a representative book so far the forms and contents of *Shroutsutras* are concerned. At most of the places, the subject is dealt in detail but when there is the need it has presented them in the most concise form. It has simplified and presented the matters of *Brahman Granthas* in an easy format for easy understanding and common use.

Kātyāyan Shroutsutra is divided into 26 chapters which include *kandikās.* The 1st chapter deals with the definitions of different articles and materials needed. 2nd and 3rd chapters deal with *Darshapurnamāsa* in detail. 4th deals with *Pindapitriyagya* etc, 5th with *Chāturmāsayāga*, 6th with *Nirudhpashubandha*, 7th to 11th with *Soma yāga*, 12th with *Dwādashah*, 13th with *Gawāmayana*, 14th with *Bājpeya*, 15th with *Rājasuya*, 16th to 18th with Selection of Fire, 19th with *Sautrāmani*, 20th with *Aswamedha*, 21st with

Purushmedha, Sarvamedha, Pitrimedha, 22nd with *Yekāh,* 23rd with *Ahinayāga,* 24th with *Satrayāga,* 25th with *Prāyashchita* (expiation), and 26th with *Pravargya.*

The Sutras of Krishna Yajur Veda

1. *Āpastamba Shroutsutra*
2. *Hiranyakesiya* or *Satyāshārha Shroutsutra*
3. *Boudhāyan Shroutsutra*
4. *Bhāradwāj Shroutsutra*
5. *Vaikhānas Shroutsutra*
6. *Vādhool Shroutsutra*
7. *Mānava Shroutsutra*
8. *Vārāh Shroutsutra*
9. *Mānava Grihyasutra*
10. *Kāthak Grihyasutra*
11. *Āpastamba Grihyasutra*
12. *Boudhāyan Grihyasutra*
13. *Vaikhānas Grihyasutra*
14. *Hiranyakesiya Grihyasutra*
15. *Mānava Dharmasutra*
16. *Kāthak Dharmasutra*
17. *Āpastamba Dharmasutra*
18. *Boudhāyan Dharmasutra*
19. *Vaikhānas Dharmasutra*
20. *Hiranyakesiya Dharmasutra*

The Sutras of Sãma Veda

1. *Masaksutra*
2. *Lãtyãyansutra*
3. *Drãhyãyansutra*
4. *Khãdir Shroutsutra*
5. *Jaiminiya Grihyasutra*
6. *Govil Grihyasutra*
7. *Khãdir Grihyasutra*
8. *Drãhyãyan Grihyasutra*
9. *Gautam Dharmasutra*

The Sutras of Atharva Veda

1. *Vaitãn Shroutsutra*
2. *Kaushika Grihyasutra*
3. *Vãrãh Grihyasutra*
4. *Vaikhãnas Grihyasutra*

Prãtisãkhya and Anukramani

Prãtisãkhya

Prãtisãkhya are the books on the rules of the use of language. They aim at teaching the correct pronunciatiations of Vedic hymns. These are the original books of phonetics. These are definitely a sort of Vedic *Vyākaran*. Different *Prātishākhya* are available in and for different Vedas. They are also called *Sulvasutra*, which are mostly the books of mathematics and science.

Kātyāyan Sulvasutra is the principal *Sulvasutra* of *Yajur Veda* which deals with geometry and explains its various facets.

The *Sulvasutras* were lost and with them the knowledge of Vedic physics and geometry too was completely lost, though the knowledge of chemistry, botany and zoology was saved to some extent in the books of Ayurveda. But in *Sanskrit Vyākaran* (Grammar) it has separate existence also.

The *Prātisākhya* of *Shukla Yajur Veda* is famous as ***Vajasneyi Prātisākhya***. Maharshi Kātyāyana has compiled it. It has 8 chapters and 734 *sutras*. In it mainly alphabet, letters, vowels and consonants, *sandhi* (synapse), recitation and sequential recitation have been discussed. There are two appendices to it: *Pratigyā Sutra* and *Bhāshika Sutra*. The former deals with the phonetics of the *Samhitās* while the latter deals with the phonetics of *Shatpatha Brahman*.

Rig Veda Prātisākhya was authored by Shaunaka while ***Taitteriya Prātisākhya*** belongs to *Krishna Yajur Veda*. *Atharva Veda* has its own *Prātisākhya* which was also compiled originally by Shaunaka as ***Shaunakiya Chatura Adhyāyikā***.

Anukramani

Anukramani are a part of *Prātisākhya.* The purpose behind these books is to save, analyse, elucidate and explain the Vedas. They provide the list according to *mantras,* or the alphabetical list of the *Chhand* (metre) or classify the *mantras* according to the *Devatās.*

The *Anukramani* of *Sāma Veda* and *Atharva Veda* are not available.

One great aspect of Vedic Literature, and thus of Sanskrit literature, is that it adds value and cosmic energy to everything, including phonetics, pronunciation and letters. Thus they make them sublime and divine.

Akshar (usually letters but in Vedas syllables also) means an imperishable entity, *swar* (vowel sound) is treated as *Prāna Akshar* (imperishable life force i.e. the soul which never dies), *vyanjana* (consonantal sound) means embellishment which are divided as *sparsa* (syllables from *ka* to *ma*), *antastha* (*ya, ra, la, va*) and *usmana* (accented *sa, sha* and unaccented *sa*). They include nasal sounds also.

It is said that a consonant in Sanskrit can be articulated in as many as 18 ways which depends entirely on time, manner and accent. Moreover, the sounds change according to the least and the most stress on a syllable or word i.e. ***hraswa, deergha*** and ***plut swar***.

Even the vowels are divided into three based on the ways of chanting and on the accent articulation. We have five places for articulation i.e. *Kanthal* (throat), *Tālabyal* (palatal), *Murdhanyal* (cerebral), *Danta Swar* (dental) and *Oshthal* (lips).

There is little wonder that sounds of alphabet and pronunciations keep on changing, which have helped in the growth of languages, words and literature.

The available *Anukramani Granthas* of *Rig Veda* are the following:

1. *Arshānukramani*
2. *Chhandonukramani*
3. *Devatanukramani*
4. *Anuvākānukramani*
5. *Sarvānukramani*
6. *Brihadaivatānukramani*
7. *Rigvigāyan*
8. *Brihad Parishishta*
9. *Shānkhāyayan Parishishta*
10. *Āswalāyan Parishishta*
11. *Rigpratishākhya*

Vedāng

The Vedas are the storehouse of all the knowledge of mankind. They present not only the creation but also the outer and inner growth, the developments of civilisations and cultures.

There are six further divisions of Vedas which facilitate their reading and understanding. In the Vedic Sanskrit, the meaning of *ang* is not body parts or organs but 'one which explains well'.

Angyante gyāyante abhibhiriti angāni

(It means the instruments which help in knowing an element.)

Since our different organs help in knowing things and recognising objects so they are deemed as *ang* justifying the meaning of the word.

The *Vedāngs* help in knowing the Vedas well. They are categorised as different *angs* of Vedas.

Vedāngs are six in number:

1. ***Shikshā***, the nose of the Vedas: *shikshā ghrānam tu vedasya.*
2. ***Kalp***, the hands of the Vedas: *hastau kalpo yasya pathyate.*
3. ***Vyākaran***, the mouth of the Vedas: *mukham vyākaranam smritam.*
4. ***Nirukta***, the ears of the Vedas: *niruktam shrotamuchayate.*
5. ***Chhand***, the feet of the Vedas: *chhandah pādau tu vedasya.*
6. ***Jyotish***, the eyes of the Vedas: *jyotishāmayanam chakshuh.*

1. Shikshā

Shikshā Granthas aim at analysing and teaching sound. They describe how to modulate and produce the sound, control it and correct the pronunciation. It emphasises on the use of *deergha* (accented) and *hraswa* (unaccented) syllables of different *mantrās*, *chhand*, *suktās* and *sutras*.

Shikshā Granthas are the most ancient and dependable books on the science of **Phonetics** and **Phonology**. There are more than 25 books mentioned at many places but the available books are very few. They are:

1. *Panineeya Shikshā* related to the *Rig Veda*
2. *Vyās Shikshā* related to the *Krishna Yajur Veda*
3. *Yāgyavalkya Shikshā* related to the *Shukla Yajur Veda*
4. *Gautami Shikshā* related to the *Sāma Veda*
5. *Lomasheeya Shikshā* related to the *Sāma Veda*
6. *Nāradeeya Shikshā* related to the *Sāma Veda*
7. *Māndooki Shikshā* related to the *Atharva Veda*

Gautami Shikshā, *Lomasheeya Shikshā* and *Nāradeeya Shikshā*, which are related to the *Sāma Veda* lay great stress on the pronunciation-system and the differences in pronunciation. All these three *shikshās* are divided into two *Prapāthakas* and sixteen *Kandikās*. They enjoy a very special place among the *Prātisākhya* literature. For the correct pronunciation of the ***Sāmas*** (which has become **Psalms** in

English, it shows their deep-rooted relation and proves that somehow every nation and its literature owe a lot to the Vedas) *Rictantras*, *Sāmatantras*, *Akshartantras* and *Pushptantras* were composed.

The *Sāmatantra,* created for learning the pronunciation and singing the Nature's songs (*Prakriti Gāna*), has been divided into 13 *Prapāthakas* but *Akshartantra* has only two *Prapāthakas* and *Pushpasutra* which analyses the *Uha. Uhya Sāma* has ten *Prapāthakas* and one hundred parts.

In *Shukla Yajur Veda,* there are many treatises on *Shikshā* but the *Yāgyavalkya Shikshā* is the most important and is usually followed. Among the *Krishna Yajur Veda's Shikshā* treatises, *Bhāradwāj Shikshā* (which is also known as *Samhitā Shikshā* and *Vāsa Shikshā* are available.

2. Kalp

Kalp Granthas discuss the ways, means and place etc for the arrangements and completion of *yajnas*. The names of the *kalps* are not available and though there are hundreds of books available, the names of all the available *granthas* are difficult to search out. Many persons are working in the direction to search out, collect and analyse all such books.

It is not difficult to understand the need of the *kalp* for there is only one reason behind the creation of different types of treatises. Whenever some difficulties were faced in understanding certain texts and in answering the inquisitive pupils and general mass then another type of book was written to fulfil that need. However, the original reason behind the creation of literature remained the same, i.e. to preserve and spread the knowledge gained and collected through different sources.

Kalpo Veda vihitānām karmnāmānupurvyena kalpana shāshtram

— *Rig Veda Prātishākhya*

(Kalp is the science of making the understanding of the truth expressed in the Vedas easier.)

So *kalp* is campared to the most useful and busy hands. There is no doubt that *kalp* is the hands of Vedas: *hastau kalpo atha kathyate.*

Kāyākalp means the metamorphosis of body. *Kalp* in itself, particularly its *sutras* have the inner power to metamorphose the mind and life of a person. The saints, the householders and others need these *Kalp Sutras* for the essential inner changes which are important in the present day context when restlessness, anxiety, fatigue and obsessions are ruling the heart and mind. We lack clear vision and definite purpose. It is our fault that we do not read these *Kalp Sutras.*

Usually *Kalp Sutras* are divided in three different categories:

- *Shroutsutra*

- *Grihyasutra*
- *Dharmasutra*

Some scholars have included *Shulvasutras* also as *Kalp Sutra's* fourth division.

Shroutsutras are for the *yajnas. Āswālāyana* and *Shankhyāyana* are two important *Shroutsutras.*

Dharmasutras are for the kings, ministers, commanders and officers. The famous *Dharmasutras* are written by Gautam, Boudhāyana, Āpastamba, Vashishtha, Hiranyakesi and Vaikhānus.

Grihyasutras are for the general masses. While performing their rituals and rites, the householders follow the *Grihyasutras.* These are the *Karmakāndas,* the basis of all rites. All the 16 *Sanskārs,* numerous *Anushthāns,* each *Reeti* and *Rasma* are performed according to the *Grihyasutras. Āswālāyana* and *Pāraskar Grihyasutras* are the most impotant ones which are the rules for a householder to lead his life and perform different *Sanskārs* in the correct manner. If we go to the extreme, then we can claim that the *Kalp Sutras* are the life-elements (*Prāna*) of *Hindutwa,* Hindu religion, Hindu civilisation and culture.

They also help in understanding the daily chores, regular rites, wholesome and unwholesome and attached and detached deeds. We have been following them since time immemorial.

1. Yajna in Kalp Sutras

The Hindus have 42 *Karmas* in all. They are: 14 *Shrout Yajna*, 7 *Pāka Yajna*, 5 *Mahā Yajna* and 16 *Sanskārs*.

All the *Kalp Sutras* combined together give the details of all these *Karmas*. Every literate Hindu should read and follow them. The growth, developments, changes which have entered our lives over the years have to be incorporated. The things must be known, the concept must be clear and the deeds generally must follow the essence of the dictates if not the words of dictates. Hindus have always survived due to their tolerance, capacity to accept changes and their flexible nature.

2. Shrout Yajnas

Seven *Haviryajna* which are performed with *Havi* are:

1. *Agnyādhāna(Agnihotra)*
2. *Nirudhpashubandha*
3. *Darshpurnamāsa*
4. *Āgrāhāyana*
5. *Chāturmāsya*
6. *Soutrāmani*
7. *Pindapitriyagya*

Seven *Somayajna* which are performed with *Soma* are:

1. *Agnistoma*
2. *Atyagnistoma*

3. *Ukthya*
4. *Shodasi*
5. *Bājpeya*
6. *Atirātra*
7. *Āptoryāma*

3. Pāka Yajnas

1. *Pitri Yajna*
2. *Pārwana Yajna* or *Purnimā Yajna*
3. *Ashtakā Yajna*
4. *Shrāvani Yajna*
5. *Āswayuji Yajna* (performed in the month of *Ashwina*)
6. *Āgrahāyani Yajna* (It has changed into harvesting festival, *Nawānna Yajna* and is performed in different regions by different names)
7. *Chaitri Yajna*

Almost all the *yajnas* have changed, both in their form and content and name and meaning but are performed with utmost devotion by the farmers and poor people whom we call *Shudras* and labourers.

4. Mahā Yajna

1. *Deva Yajna*
2. *Bhoota Yajna*

3. *Pitri Yajna*
4. *Brahma Yajna*
5. *Manusya Yajna*

5. Sanskārs

1. *Garbhādhāna*
2. *Punswan*
3. *Seemāntoanayan*
4. *Jātakarma*
5. *Nāmakaran*
6. *Niskramana*
7. *Annaprāshana*
8. *Vapankriyā*
9. *Upanayan*
10. *Karnabedha*
11. *Keshant*
12. *Vedārambh*
13. *Vedasnān*
14. *Vivāh*
15. *Vivāhgniparigrah*
16. *Tretāgnisangrah*

These 16 *Sanskārs* have also been mentioned in the chapters on *Smritis* because *Smritis* too are the real Hindu Scriptures. The world of Vedas includes both pure sciences and applied sciences which have been divided in *Shruti* and *Smriti.*

Despite the fact that the *rishis* have asked all to perform the *yajnas* designated for them, they have laid ample stress on only truth, virtues, good qualities and pure deeds. In absence of these traits in a human, all the *yajnas* performed by him will go in vain. Those who possess these sublime qualities will get salvation and be sent to Heaven.

It is said in the *Vashishtha Dharmasutra* (6:3): "*As after getting wings the birds fly out and forsake their nest, in the same manner the Vedas and the Vedangs forsake the men without virtues.*"

All the *Kalp Sutras* of each Veda have been planned and written in different ways; and describe different *yajnas* and *Karma* but the *Sutras* of one particular Veda have many similarities and have been planned and written on a similar pattern. The *Kalp Sutras* of *Rig Veda* discuss Vedic *yajnas.* There is similarity in each *Shroutsutra* and again in each *Grihyasutra* but these two *sutras* are entirely different.

Only *Āpastamba Kalp Sutras* are really different but only in technique not in content. Sage Āpastamba was born in Andhra Pradesh and is very popular in South India. In fact, the Dravidians and Tailang Brahmins treat themselves as descendants of Āpastamba's family.

3. Vyākaran

The books of *Vyākaran* or the Grammar give a definite shape, order and meaning to the language used and the ideas expressed. There are many purposes behind the study of Grammar.

- Grammar helps in keeping the existing knowledge safe and in its understanding.
- It gives the power to think new things and create new imagery.
- It sharpens and corrects the language and makes both the intellect and imagination fertile.
- It teaches the proper usage of words.
- It makes one refined, civilised and cultured.
- It helps in condensation of ideas.
- It gives compactness to language.
- It removes all the doubts.

Hence, Grammar is the most important thing to study:

एकः शब्दः सम्यग् ज्ञातः शास्त्रान् वितः।
सुप्रयुक्तः स्वर्गे लोके च कामधुग् भवति।।

Ekah shabdah samyag gyātah shāshtrānwitah
suprayuktah swarge loke cha kāmdhug bhawati

(If you use one word in its most appropriate place then one succeeds in this world and goes up to heaven.)

In Sanskrit, the *Vyākaran* by Pānini is the most famous one. The disciples and the scholars all imbibe the whole book and all the *sutras* by heart. Pānini's *Ashtādhyāyi* or *Siddhanta Kaumudi*, both *Laghu* (condensed) and *Brihad* (complete) and the *Vyākaran* by Shāktāyan seem to be related to *Yajur Veda*.

In fact, it was Panini who collected, edited, modified and enlarged all other *sutras* available till then, and his book is so complete in itself that the scholars did not feel the need for any other treatise.

Panini is believed to have been the incarnation of *Sheshnāg*. He was asked to compile Grammar. He did it in a secluded camp where the women were not allowed to go. He used to write the book in the form of *Sheshnāg*. Once, by chance, a woman entered the camp. It was his last day. He disappeared and the end of the book, the concluding *sutra*, remained incomplete. *Mahābhāshya* by Maharshi Pātanjali and Kātyāyan are two unique books on Grammar still available which explain Panini's *sutras*.

Panini's Grammar consists of four parts:

Part 1. ***Shivasutra*** — Phonology, the notations for phonemes

Part 2. ***Ashtadhyāyi*** — Morphology, construction rules for complexes

Part 3. ***Dhātupada*** — List of Roots, classes of verbal roots

Part 4. ***Ganapada*** — General, it provides lists of primitive nominal stems

Only a handful of other Grammar treatises are available. Some of them are following:

1. *Vyākaran* by Pānini — *Siddhānta Kaumudi*
2. *Shāktāyan Vyākaran*
3. *Sāraswata Vyākaran*
4. *Kāmdhenu Vyākaran*
5. *Hemchandra Vyākaran*
6. *Prākrit Prakāsh*
7. *Prākrit Vyākaran*
8. *Kalāp Vyākaran*
9. *Mugdha-bodha Vyākaran*

4. Nirukta

The *Nirukta Granthas* are the encyclopaedias of the Vedas. A *Nirukta Grantha* consists of brief rules in the form of *sutras* for deriving meanings. It is supplemented with a glossary of difficult and rare Vedic words. Only three such books are said to be available. I have seen only one by Yāskāchārya who is so popular that he has become synonymous to *Nirukta* and is mostly held as the author of *Niruktas*. The reason may be the popularity of his *Veda-Bhãshya* and the commentary on *Nighantu*. There is yet another reason stated for the loss of the books.

It is claimed that due to the loss of the lives of learned Brahmins there were few left to protect these books. They were not able to memorise all the treatises on Grammar and the encyclopaedias of the Vedas. Just like after the great popularity of Panini's *Vyãkaran*, rest of the *Vyãkarans* were not taken care of, in the same way after the popularity of Yãskãchãrya's book, others lost importance. While the truth is that so many great gurus were massacred such that the very generation of the *rishis*, *munis* and *ãchãryãs* came to an end and there was none left to protect and use these great books.

In order to lure the general mass to come in the open to protect these books, many such statements were added that can show the immediate profit of reading and memorising the *Samhitãs* and other *Granthas*.

For example:

(a) ***Kãlindi samhitã gyeyã*** — The recitation of *Samhitãs* gives the virtues of bathing in the river Yamunã

(b) ***Samhitã nayate suryapadam*** — By reciting the *Samhitãs* one gets to the world of the sun

(c) ***Padamuktã Saraswati*** — The recitation gives the benefits of taking bath in the secret river Saraswati

The long period of Indian slavery is the period of the loss of human knowledge, hence, of the greatest loss to humanity. The rulers tried hard to uproot and wipe out Indian culture and civilisation with all cruelty and strength. There is yet another aspect of human life, luxury and philosophy that cannot be ignored. During the last few centuries, man as a whole has been talking about toughness of task and labour, tension and the ways to reduce it. He has grown very weak and is still growing weaker, hence is unable to cope with the concentration, devotion, dedication and labour required for acquiring such great, divine and secret knowledge. The modern man surrounded by all sorts of distracting elements cannot get the needed meditative concentration. The result is that the Indians are dependent on other countries for their own knowledge.

The three available *Nirukta Granthas* are the following:

1. *Yāskāchārya Nirukta*
2. *Kashyap Nirukta*
3. *Shākpooni Nirukta*

Sāyanāchārya, in the preface to *Chaturveda Bhāshya*, has written:

Arthāwabodhe nirpekshtayā padjātam yatroktam tanniruktam

(It is Nirukta if compiled with detachment in the conception of meaning wherever the etymology of syllables has been written.)

The clear meaning of *Nirukta* is 'that which is said/ written without prejudices.' *Nirukta* explains the hidden and inner meaning of the Vedas while other treatises aim at the general meaning of the *mantras*. Others are written in *suktas* while *nirukta* is written in prose.

In a way, *Nirukta* is a commentary on *Nighantu Granthas* which explain the difficult words of the Vedas. They are said to be the dictionaries of Vedas.

According to the *Moksha-Dharma-Parva* of the *Mahābhārata*, original *Nighantu* was written by Prajāpati Kashyap. The available *Nirukta* by Yāskāchārya is claimed to have been written at a later date but it cannot be possible since he has been mentioned as the writer of *Nirukta* in the *Shānti Parva* of the *Mahābhārata*. He was definitely a contemporary of *Ved Vyās*. He has mentioned twelve writers of *Niruktas*.

There are twelve chapters in the *Nirukta* by Yāskāchārya and two chapters as appendices. In modern language, *Nirukta* is a book of 'Linguistic' which is developing in western countries for the past hundred years or so. That is one reason that after the famous speech of Vivekanand in Chicago, the general comment was:

"Where western thinking ends, the Indians have started to think."

It can easily be imagined how far, deep and high they have gone during that period of deep meditation. That is the reason that a comparison is not possible in the height, depth, sublimity and divinity with Indian thinking and knowledge. One can see the list of inventions, through which Europe made its presence felt, came up only after Vasco da Gama (He came to Calicut in 1488 AD. Before that there is not a single invention from Europe.) discovered the sea-route to India and returned back with collection of books as gifts from India.

5. Chhand

Chhands are the metres for composing poetry. The books on *chhand* fix, direct and explain the different *chhands* possible and used.

There are two ways of counting the syllables in *chhand* — *Varnik* and *Mātrika.*

In ***Varnik***, the *varnas* or the letters are counted to fix the metre. It is the way the Vedas have been composed.

In ***Mātrika***, the syllables are counted on the basis of accented (*deergha mātrā*) and unaccented syllables (*hraswa mātrā*). Most of the epics of Sanskrit count the syllables on this pattern which is usually called *Laukika Chhand.*

According to Yāska, the root of *chhand* is *chhad dhātu.* The most common definition of *chhand* is: *chhandāsi chhandah* (that which covers as a canopy).

The *chhands* in Sanskrit literature are so important that Durgāchārya claimed:

Nāchchhandasi vāguchcharati

(Words are not pronounced without chhands)

On the other hand Āchārya Bharat wrote in his *Nātyashāstram:*

Chhandoheeno na shabdoasti na Chhandah shabd varjitam

(There is no word which has no chhand and chhand cannot exist without words)

Āchārya Pingal wrote *Chhand Sutra* and established the art of metrical composition in classical criticism. Other *rishis* who have worked on *chhands* are Patanjali, Shaunak and Kātyāyana.

There is mention of seven other writers of *Chhand Granthas* whose works are not available. Those writers are: Koushtuki, Yāska, Tāndi, Saitava, Kāshyapa, Shākalya and Māndaba.

Vedic *chhands* have been discussed even in such treatises whose main theme is something else. Such treatises are *Nidāna*, *Prātisākhya*, *Sarvānukramani* and *Agnipurāna.*

Primarily the following books of *chhands* are known:

1. *Gārgyaprokt Upnidānsutra* related to the *Sāma Veda*
2. *Chhandovichit Pingalnāgprokt Chhandsutra* by Pingala

3. *Chhandokramani* by Venkat Mādhav
4. *Chhandsutra* by Jaidev
5. *Halāyuddhavriti*
6. *Chhandmanjari*
7. *Vritaratnākar*
8. *Shrutabodha*
9. *Jānashrayee Chhandovichita*
10. *Jaideva Chhand*
11. *Venkat Mādhava: Chhando Anukramani*

Vedic Chhand

In the *Sarvānukramani*, Kātyāyana has defined Vedic *chhand* as:

Yadaksharparimānam tatchhandah

(Chhand is where letters are the scale of measurement)

It is clear that in Vedic *chhands* letters are counted, and *mātrās* are not given importance. In Vedas, there is no binding of *Laghu-Guru-Mātrās* (unaccented and accented syllables).

Despite the difference in opinion it is held that there are 26 Vedic *chhands*. They are described in detail in the first four chapters of *Pingal Chhandsutra*.

The following five *chhands* known as ***Gāyatri Purva Panchak*** have not been used in *Mantra Samhitās*. They are:

1. *Mā* (4 lettered)
2. *Pramā* (8 lettered)

3. *Pratimã* (12 lettered)

4. *Upamã* (16 lettered)

5. *Samã* (30 lettered)

The following thirteen *chhands* have been vehementally used in the *Rig Veda Mantra Samhitã*. They are:

1. *Gãyatri* (24 lettered)

2. *Ushnik* (28 lettered)

3. *Anushtup* (32 lettered)

4. *Brihati* (36 lettered)

5. *Pankti* (40 lettered)

6. *Trishtup* (44 lettered)

7. *Jagati* (48 lettered)

8. *Atijagati* (52 lettered)

9. *Shakwari* (56 lettered)

10. *Atishakwari* (60 lettered)

11. *Ashthi* (64 lettered)

12. *Atyashthi* (68 lettered)

13. *Dhriti* (72 lettered)

In the *Yajur Veda*, there are examples of rare *chhands* containing 76 letters to 104 letters. It is a wonder in itself. 8 such *chhands* are being given here:

S.No.	Name of *Chhand*	Number of letters	From *Yajur Veda*
1.	*Atidhriti*	76	22:5
2.	*Kriti*	80	9:32
3.	*Prakriti*	84	15:16
4.	*Ākriti*	88	15:64
5.	*Vikriti*	92	15:15
6.	*Sankriti*	96	24:1-2
7.	*Abhikriti*	100	26:1
8.	*Utakriti*	104	11:58

A total of 261 kinds of *chhands* have been used in all the *Veda Samhitās*. The following five *chhands* have been used only in the *Atharva Veda*.

S.No.	Name of *Chhand*	Number of letters	From *Atharva Veda*
1.	*Uktā*	4	2:129:8
2.	*Atyuktā*	8	2:129:1
3.	*Madhyā*	12	20:129:13
4.	*Pratishthā*	16	20:131:5
5.	*Supratishthā*	20	20:134:2

6. Jyotish

Jyotish deals with other aspects of the *yajnas* which are actually the study of the Universe, Cosmos and the life and its survival in it. The literal meaning of *Jyotish* is light heavenly body.

It is the sixth elucidatory organ of the Vedas and the most ancient Indian scientific system of studying the stars, the *Nakshatras* (constellations), zodiac signs, the *Akāsh Gangas* (galaxies), *Grahas* (planets), their movements, inter-planetary positions and the resultant effect on the earth and the life on it. It studies the time in accordance with the movements of the planets.

The names of all the books on *Jyotish* are not available. Even today, many people are writing books on Astrology and Astronomy but almost all of them are following the western pattern which is claimed to be the most scientific, but in reality it touches only the surface. The calculations in Indian *Jyotish* are correct to *Vipal* (a part of a second). The Indian Astrologers calculate even *nawamānsh* and *yayanānsh.*

Some misunderstanding towards Indian *Jyotish* and fascination towards western culture are the two basic reasons why Indian *Jyotish* is relegated to the backseat or it is better to say that it has been dethroned. The fact is that *Jyotish* everywhere is obviously the gift of Vedas. They have made some reasonable changes in Indian *Jyotish* and have adopted it and claimed it to be better. First the Europeans boasted of having discovered the ninth planet then suddenly they were not sure of their own discovery of more than hundred years old ninth planet whereas Indians have claimed nine planets since time immemorial. On most of the occasions, they substantiate the knowledge of the *rishis* and claim the benefits of new discovery. On such occasions, they try to redefine the very word 'planet', as if they are the authority on the subject and the entire solar system must move according to their dictates and wishes. They are bent upon proving the ancient *rishis* wrong who claimed *navagraha,* by displacing Pluto.

Ancient Indians claimed two movements of the Sun, *Dakshināyan* and *Uttarāyana,* which the western Astronomers confirmed only in the late 20th century.

The tropical zodiac is used in Indian Astrology to predict the seasons and rain, which the western metereologists started doing only in the 19th century.

Indian *Jyotish* is behind the development of geometry which has been discussed in ***Shulvasutras.***

The climax of Indian *Jyotish* is the division of planets in *Kārakagraha* and *Pāpagraha* — favourable and unfavourable planets.

In this way, somehow the westerners are claiming the credit for everything that the Vedas have given to the world.

In ancient past, Indian astrologers and sculptors went to many countries, in wild and wide deserts, and made the replicas of the night-sky. One such replica is in China and another was found a decade back somewhere in Egypt. In all probabilities, it was constructed first in India but due to the changing courses of various rivers it has been lost and has not been found anywhere in India.

One great difference between Indian and western *Jyotish* is that western *Jyotish* calculates only the months, at the most the fortnight, while Indian *Jyotish* through *Jogini* calculations calculates *Nakshatra*, date, 4 parts of a day, hour, minute and seconds. That is how they successfully calculate the solar and lunar eclipses of hundred or more than hundred years ahead with unparalleled accuracy. That is why it is said to be *Kālavigyāpaka Shāstra* (the science of calculating time). Nowadays its use is mostly limited to calculating the *Muhurat* — the most suitable time for doing an auspicious work or marriage. While in the past, even the best time for copulation was calculated for bearing brilliant and healthy sons. It was done so because our success depends not only on our best efforts but also on the balanced energy from all the Elements that we get from the Cosmos. *Karma* and *bhāgya* are the real parents. The birth is not possible without their union.

वेदा हि यज्ञार्थामाभिप्रवृत:,
कालाभिपूर्व विहितानश्च यज्ञा:।
तस्मादिदं कालाविधानाशास्त्रम्,
यो ज्योतिष वेद स वेद यज्ञम्।।

Vedā hi yagyārthamabhiprabritāh
Kālābhipurba vihitānshcha yagyāh

Tasmādidam kālavidhānashāshtram
Yo Jyotish Veda sa Veda yagyam

(The success of yajnas depends not only on accurately performaning the rituals but in performing them when the positions of the constellations and planets are favourable to get balanced Yoga or union.)

Some people foster a wrong notion that *Jyotish* is a later development and it is not in the *Veda Samhitās* but during Vedic age each of the four Vedas had their separate *Jyotish.* Unfortunately, the *Jyotish* of *Sāma Veda* is not available these days but others still have their *Jyotish Shāstra* composed in verse form:

- ***Rig Veda*** *Ārcha Jyotish* 36 verses
- ***Yajur Veda*** *Yājush Jyotish* 39 verses
- ***Atharva Veda*** *Ātharvana Jyotish* 162 verses

Jyotish is very fast and deep and high as it includes Astrology, Astronomy, Cosmology, Astrophysics and Space-science. The following are some of the famous *granthas* on *Jyotish*:

1. *Vedāng Jyotish* by Lagadhāchārya
2. *Jyotish* by Nārad
3. *Jyotish Grantha* by Parāsher
4. *Jyotish Grantha* by Vashishtha
5. *Jyotish* by Varāhmihir
6. *Jyotish* by Āryabhatta

7. *Jyotish* by Bhãskarãchãrya
8. *Jyotish* by Brahmagupta

Upa-vedas

Every Veda has an Upa-veda and some related *granthas* on those Upa-vedas.

Rig Veda — Arthaveda

The Upa-veda of *Rig Veda* is *Arthaveda.* It is mostly related to Economics. The book by Brihaspati is accepted as very old and that of Kautilya is said to have been written after a gap of many centuries.

A few famous ones are given below:

1. *Brihaspateh Arthãdhikãrikam*
2. *Kautilya's Arthashãstra*
3. *Nitivãkyãmritasutra* by Somdevbhatta
4. *Chãnakya Sutra*
5. *Kãmandak Sutra*
6. *Shukraniti*

Yajur Veda — Dhanurveda

The Upa-veda of *Yajur Veda* is *Dhanurveda,* which is mostly related to the manufacture of arms and weapons. They also teach how to use the weapons.

When Sri Krishna achieved total disarmament then these weapons were allowed to the people to use in self-defence. Vaishampāyan's book is treated as the best in this regard.

These are the few very famous books on *Dhanurveda*:

1. *Vaishampāyan Nitiprakāshika*
2. *Vriddha Shārandhar*
3. *Yuktikalptaru*
4. *Samarāngan Sutradhār*

Sāma Veda — Gandharvaveda

The Upa-veda of *Sāma Veda* is *Gandharvaveda.* The books of *Gandharvaveda* are mostly related to music and the art of singing and dancing. They are the books on classical music and aim solely at the practice of *Nād Brahman*. They deal with all types of *Rāgas* and *Rāginis*, musical instruments, types of dances, dresses and other such aspects in detail. They are known by *Gharānā*. It is claimed that at present there is no singer of the two great ways of *Sāmgān* known as *Arnyagān* and *Geyagān*.

The following are some famous books on this great art of music, singing and dancing:

1. *Natyashastram* by Bharatmuni
2. *Dattilam* by Dattilmuni
3. *Sangeet Ratnakar* by Shārangdev

4. *Mallināth Ratnākar* by Mallināth
5. *Sangeet Darpan* by Dāmodar

Atharva Veda — Āyurveda

The Upa-veda of *Atharva Veda* is *Āyurveda* which deals with general physiology and hygiene. In the books of *Āyurveda* the diseases, their causes, symptoms, herbal medicines and preventive measures have been discussed. It is a great science and has not as yet been surpassed by any other form of treatment. The medicines prepared and prescribed in it have virtually no side-effect for they are all based on natural things particularly herbs and juices. The ***Nighantus***, books on Botany and other chemicals found from different plants, must also be included in this category. But somehow they have not been mentioned in it.

Birth of Āyurveda

There are many tales about the birth of *Āyurveda* but all the tales lead to Brahmā who after creating the Vedas, created the Upa-vedas and *Vedāngs*. Among them was the most needed *Āyurveda*. After creating *Āyurveda*, Brahmā gave it to the Sun. From the original, he composed an independent *Samhitā* and gave it to his disciples. Then it got associated with many learned *rishis* and *yogis* who spread this science of treatment. Those who got associated with it in the most ancient time are: Dhanwantari, Kāsirāja, Divodāsa, Aswinikumārs, Nakul, Sahdeo, Suryaputra Yama, Chyavana, Janaka, Buddha, Jābāla, Jājali, Paila, Karatha and Agastya. They were all experts in knowing the diseases and their causes, in preparing herbal medicines, and in eradicating the disease from its root.

Dhanwantari was so great in this field that he is always addressed as *Bhagwan Dhanwantari*. He wrote ***Chikitsā Tatwa Vigyāna***. Kāsirāja followed in his footsteps and wrote ***Divya Chikitsā Kaumudi*** and Divodāsa wrote ***Chikitsā Darpana***.

Both the Aswinikumārs in a joint effort produced another great book, ***Chikitsā Sāratantra***. The most wonderful thing about them is that all these treatises were produced in exquisite poetic form myriads of years back.

Thousands of years after these books were written, the Battle of Mahābhārata was fought and two sons of Pandu — Nakul and Sahdeo wrote two great books. Nakul wrote ***Vaidaka Sarvaswa*** and Sahadeo came up with ***Vyādhisindhuvimardan***.

Yama, the God of death and the son of Surya, wrote ***Gānārnava***.

Chyavana Rishi wrote the book ***Jeevan Dāna***.

The famous Yogi and Sita's father Videha Janaka wrote ***Vaidyasandehabhanjana***, the book which erases the doubts of the doctors.

Buddha gave ***Sarva Sāra***, Jābāla gave ***Tantra Sāra*** and Jājali Muni gave ***Vedāna Sāra.***

Three more books were added during that time. They were ***Nidāna Tantra*** by Paila, ***Sarvadhar Tantra*** by Karatha, and ***Dwaidha Nirnaya*** by none but the famous Rishi Agastya who had drunk the sea in anger.

The books of *Āyurveda* are very ancient and mentioned with great respect in Indian society. They are:

1. *Aswinikumār Samhitā*
2. *Brahman Samhitā*
3. *Bhela Samhitā*
4. *Āgnighrasutraraj*
5. *Sushruta Samhitā*
6. *Dhātuvad*
7. *Dhanwantarisutra*
8. *Mānsutra*
9. *Soopasutra*
10. *Sauvarisutra*
11. *Dālabhyasutra*
12. *Jābālisutra*
13. *Indrasutra*
14. *Shabdakautuhal*
15. *Devalsutra*
16. *Charak Samhitā*
17. *Ashtānghridaya*

○○

4

Vedas and Smritis — Hindu Scriptures

Hindu religion and the Hindu society is guided thoroughly, completely and comprehensively by the great *Smriti Granthas* which deal with all the four main deeds of a human being. They are really very famous and essential. ***Dharma, Artha, Kāma*** and ***Moksha*** form the main subject matter of all the *smritis* because these explain the main works and working fields of human beings.

Smritis

Smritis deal with the cosmic system, the working of nature and the creation of all the living and the non-living beings. They work as the eyes and mind of all:

Pitridevamanushyanām vedaschakshu sanātanam

(Vedas work as eternal eyes)

Smritis are divided in the following categories:

1. *Smriti Granthas*
2. *Purānas*

3. *Itihās*
4. *Darshan*
5. *Nibandh Granthas*
6. *Āgam Granthas*
7. *Nitishāstra*

Vedas have worked as eyes to the original and parental gods and our forefathers, which always guide the humanity. That is one reason why they are eternal, and deal with the inner working of the whole Universe. The system that rules the Universe has been said to be 'self-born' and 'eternal'. In the same way, God too is 'self-born' and 'eternal'. Because of definite prejudices, the attackers declared them first as Hindu scriptures but later they painstakingly divided them and declared that they are all *Brahman Granthas*. But the fact is that as all other religions are based on them, so Hinduism is also based on that Eternal Religion.

Almost everything in Hindu religion is based on the *Smriti Granthas* which claim that even after the extinction of the present creation, the Vedas, the *Shruti* and the *Smriti Granthas* will remain and as they have guided the Creator, gods and men in the past, they will again and again guide them to create, procreate and sustain the Universe. In the absence of the Vedas, it would be difficult to fix the 'works and duties' of every 'being' because everything moves on the designated path of the earlier epochs: ***yathāpurvamkalpyeta.***

Smritis are the great treatises which were written by Brahma and other *rishis* with the help of their memory when the revelation and the vision of the Vedas were over. They recollected all and wrote them in their own words. So, in meaning, form and substance, the *Smritis* are like the Vedas. The only difference is that they are the words of *rishis*. Another difference is that the words, meaning and the pronunciation of the *Shrutis* get renewed in every epoch but only the meaning in *Smritis* gets renewed. They are almost equal in status. The greatness of the *Smritis* lies in the fact that they explain, elucidate and clarify many 'secrets and meanings' of the *mantras* of Vedas which would not be otherwise clear. In their absence, they would have remained ambiguous. They are the two sides of the same coin and they balance each other well. It is clearly interdependence, hence the study of the *Smritis* is made compulsory after the study of the Vedas or the *Shrutis*. It is said in the *Aitareya Samhitā* that the disciple, student or the scholar who does not read the *Smritis* after learning Vedas remains an 'animal' and takes birth as an animal 21 times in his later lives:

वेदं गृहीत्वा यः कश्चिच्छास्त्रां चैवावमन्यते।
स सद्यः पशुनां याति संभावनेकविंशतिम्।।

Vedam gribitwā yah kashchidchhāstrām chaivāvamanyate
Sa sadyah pashunam yāti sambhāvanekavinshatim

— *Aitareya Samhitā* (1:11)

Out of the two eyes that we have, one is the *Shruti* and the other is the *Smriti*. One cannot feel the sense of perfection or even completeness in the absence of any one. Those who do not possess either of the two are completely blind:

श्रुतिस्मृतीतु विप्राणां चक्षुशी द्वे विनिर्मिते।
काणस्तत्रैकया हीनो द्वाभ्यामन्धाः प्रकीर्तितः॥

Shrutismrititu biprānām chakshushi dwe vinirmite
Kānastatraiukayā hino dwābhyāmandhah prakirtitah

— *Vadhulsmriti* (190:191)

Importance of Smritis

The knowledge is accepted to be in the Vedas and the scriptures have come out of the *Smritis*:

श्रुतिस्तु वेदो विज्ञेयो धर्मशास्त्रं तु वै स्मृतिः।

Shrutiastu vedo vigyeyo dharmashāstram
tu wai smritih

Both of them are the gifts of the Supreme God. Hence they are for all. Knowingly or unknowingly, the whole world follows, some consciously and the rest in their subconscious. If a man has some reason and intellect, he has something of them. Most of them are rigid and foolish enough to deny them and divide them for their own material gain. They forget that the existence of the Universe, the earth and the life on it does not depend on the 'money and matter' that man has created. They all exist by and depend on the 'eternal and undercurrent system' behind the Universe, on the cosmic energy and life-element that each living and non-living (in our eyes only) draws from those natural elements and resources. Many Western countries wrongly believe that they can take the resources out of the earth and store them in their arsenal and godowns for their own use. They must and immediately realise that those things are well saved, protected and rejuvenated by Nature. Man cannot store them because the forces of Nature are bound to destroy them, for it is the natural and eternal law. Those who have arrogantly and wildly created nuclear weapons are now worried about their storage. They are thinking to keep them in the Space where there are greater dangers because of the incessant frictions and meteors. They are dumping the nuclear garbage inside the earth and seas without worrying about the leakage which can prove fatal to all life forms in later years when they themselves will not be there to see or face the devastation, total destruction or complete annihilation. They promise not to use the nuclear weapons, then why are they manufacturing? Is it only to terrorise other human beings or to get the Universe destroyed at a later stage? On the other hand, the Vedas, the *Shrutis* and the *Smritis* deal with the problems related to the health, peace, happiness and continuity of the earth and the life on it. The *rishis* were more worried about the future of their progeny – the great grandchildren of their great grandchildren.

They had no worry about their own self which they claimed to be an ordinary and temporary cover, a case to keep life intact and to make it grow perfect. Some people say that the morose western attitude has harmed India and Indian people. It is only the half-truth. The truth is that it is destroying all — the countries, the governments and the people who are manufacturing weapons for mass destruction on a large scale and the people, so-called terrorists, who are indiscriminately using them, apparently to kill some and terrorise many but unknowingly both of them are destroying life, nature and other life-sustaining elements. They are all a big, bold and dangerous question mark on the very existence of life. They are causing greater harm to themselves. India knows how to live with the least in the open lap of Nature. Its tropical climate also helps in it. It is really a great problem for those who live in extreme climates and need greater protection from the wild nature, cold, snowfall, tornadoes or desert heat. They will have to be cool and think and re-think about their own deeds. They must repeatedly search the answer to the question, **"Whom are they destroying?"**

Therefore, before attempting to come to a final answer they must know the essence of these *Smritis* which will definitely guide them and pave the eternal way, the way which can save all including the Universe, the Cosmos and the planets and the stars.

Number of Smritis

There are more than hundred *Smritis* still available. In the chapter, many of them will be mentioned and their important theological and religious concept will be discussed. One must go through at least two of them before fixing one's own aims and objectives and the duties towards the self and the Universe. *Smritis* discuss *Dharma, Artha, Kāma* and *Moksha* in detail because they form the basis of our duties and because we work to get them and possess them. They lay due stress on the four different stages of life, discuss particular work in a particular season or at a particular ceremony, ways to purify oneself and ways to rule. They have created laws and punishments and have shown the way to salvation or *nirvāna.*

Though ***Parāshersmriti*** has been accepted as the best guide for the *Kaliyug*, the two most important among the *Smritis* are ***Manusmriti*** and ***Yāgyavalkyasmriti*** which have thought over, fixed and designated our duties in detail. They have a lot of essence in them for they are mostly based on the general, normal, abnormal and peculiar nature, psychology and behaviour of the human beings who possess different mental power, agility and skill, and can perform different physical activities or do different and distinguished mental or menial works. Naturally they have been divided into groups and classes.

The next chapter presents a list of very important and popular books. *Itihās* and *Purānas*, also form parts of *Shruti*. It can never claim to be closer to completeness. It will simply give an insight into the rich treasure of the great treatises that the most fertile, pious and divine human brain realised in vision with the help and blessing of the God. They are so divine and godly and exquisite that they cannot be the thought of great human beings. For producing such divine things one must possess an illuminated mind. Those *rishis* and sages had their vision and revelations to give them a shape to the envisioned cosmic truth and collect them wisely and well for the benefit of posterity.

OO

5

Smriti-Granthas

Hinduism in particular (because the world says so) and all the religions taking birth in Asia or Indian subcontinent, in general, take everything for their scriptures from the *Smritis*. It is nowhere mentioned as 'Hindu *Dharmashāstra*'. But when the wise men of India mentioned them, they claimed them to be just *Dharmashāstra,* not the *Dharmashāstras* of the Hindus. At all the places, it is only *Dharmashāstra*. The Hindus are not mean-minded to claim the universal and eternal knowledge as 'only their own'. They are for all. For they claim that they are '*sarvasya vidhānsya*', the laws for all.

There are so many other things in the scriptures or the *smritis* but basically they lay great stress on the following three fundamental things.

(i) Moral Conduct

(ii) Social Behaviour

(iii) Expiation

In the scriptures, the *sutras* also play an important role. They are the laws of the governance of the world:

shāsanāchchhansanāchshāstram. Naturally, the word 'LAW' (*vidhānsya*) has been used for the Vedas. These scriptures deal with the worldly and spiritual rights and duties of man. There are twenty authentic *Smriti Granthas.* The description of ten among them is given here:

1. Manusmriti

The self-originated Manu learnt one lakh *slokas* of Vedas from his father Brahma, the Creator and taught them to his ten spiritual sons born out of his mind. Those *maharshis* heard the Vedas and taught them to their disciples; and thus the tradition of Vedas was created and carried on.

Manu too has a tradition and many incarnations. The Manus are seven in all. *Swāyambhuva* was the first and six more followed him in his tradition. They are i. *Swārochish* ii. *Uttam* iii. *Tāmas* iv. *Raiwat* v. *Chākchhush* and vi. *Vaivawasta.* The things that they taught has been collected and written by many *rishis.* Two of them, *Nārdeeya Manusmriti* and *Bhrigu Manusmriti* are more popular and authentic. The former, the *Nārdeeya,* deals with human behaviour while the latter deals with all the parts and organs of religion. It has elaborated the four main fields and deeds: *Dharma, Artha, Kāma* and *Moksha.* Naturally, *Manusmriti* is treated as the most authentic one and anything that alters the 'rule' declared by Manu is not accepted.

Everything was there given by the Lord. The one great contribution of Manu is that he collected, edited and placed everything systematically in different categories. He himself accepts it:

सर्वेषां तु स नामानि कर्माणि च पृथक् पृथक्।
वेदशब्देभ्य: एवादौ पृथक् संस्थाश्च निर्ममे।।

Serbesām tu sa nāmāni karmāni cha prithak-prithak Vedashabdebhya yewadou prithak sansthāscha nirmame

— *Manusmriti* (1:21)

As an answer to the questions of the *maharshis* in the very beginning of *Manusmriti*, Manu (Swāyambhuva Manu) explains in 58 *slokas* the first ever inundation and fresh creation out of it by the Absolute Lord. It symbolically presents and proves Creation to be the first religious, natural and pious duty of every living being. The presence of water is accepted as essential for Creation. *Creation is synthesising, joining with and at synapse many different organs and systems to function as one 'whole' or one greater system. Creation is not breaking into pieces as envisaged by the Western thinkers who gave the theory of 'Big Bang'.*

After that, Swāyambhuva Manu declares that his learned disciple Maharshi Bhrigu will tell the complete *Manusmriti*. Maharshi Bhrigu starts with the description and calculation of 'Time'. The various chapters of *Manusmriti* deal with the following facts:

1. The creation of the Universe

2. Rituals related to baptism, obeying the rules of celibacy and service to the guru
3. Entrance to worldly affairs, types of marriages, ways of the last rites
4. Ways and means to earn livelihood
5. Eatables, non-eatables, physical purity after death, the duties of women
6. The 3rd and 4th phases of life (*vānprastha and sanyās*) and salvation (*moksha*)
7. The rights and duties of a king
8. The loan and its repayment, examination of a witness
9. Duties and rights of a couple living together or separated, division of wealth, the ways to save valuables from the thieves, the rights and duties of *Vaishyas* and *Shudras*
10. Illegitimate child, duties in emergency
11. Expiation (*prāyashchita*) and its ways
12. The life of each *varna* or class on the earth, self-revelation, the works which should not be done, characteristics of each caste, and even directions regarding the blasphemous people

The following are some least discussed facts from *Manusmriti* which are important and significant, and give insight on all the four areas — personal, social, psychological and spiritual.

Omkãr and Gãyatri Mantra: In *Manusmriti,* there is a lot of stress on the *Prãtah vandanã* (morning prayer) *and Sãndhya prãrthanã* (evening prayer) mostly through *Omkãr* and *Gãyatri Mantra.* Obviously it seems like an exaggeration when one finds the statement that if one fails to read all the Vedas then he can learn *Gãyatri Mantra* and it will be equivalent to the whole Vedas. The point is that *Gãyatri* is the most difficult *mantra* to get hold of and a very hard nut to crack. During the last four or five centuries there was not a single personality who showed the knowledge of the secret symbolic meaning and hidden algebraic significance of the each letter of the *Gãyatri Mantra. Certainly, its recitation, which gives inner light, is a different thing and its symbolic scientific meaning, which throws light on the sunrays and their various uses in various forms, is quite a different act.* The *rishis* have always laid stress on the recitation of Veda *mantra* at different hours but are silent about their symbolic meaning because they are deliberately written in secret ways to avoid their misuse by unscrupulous beings.

Manusmriti asks to recite *Gãyatri Mantra* a thousand times a day and claims that the three *mahãvyãhritiyãn* (the three parts) along with the *Omkãr* known as ***Tripada Gãyatri*** are the mouth (the main part) of the Vedas and imperishable. They open the way for the union with the *Brahman* which is in effect the fusion of bodily electromagnetic power and waves with the cosmic electromagnetic power and waves. It is the very basis of the modern Information Technology.

Elders (the father and uncle) and Youngster (the son): *Manusmriti* expresses the view that an ignorant old man, who may be the father or the uncle, is like the son of a very young man who has become crystal-like learned figure of Vedas. This fact was explained by the gods when the young and learned son of Rishi Ãnagiras taught his uncles who were elder in both the relation as well as age, and started calling them 'son'. They raised objections and the clarification was sought and given.

Salutation, greetings and blessing: There is the rule of salutation to all the elders, man or woman, known or unknown. All the equals must be greeted and all the younger ones must be showered blessings. The form of each has been discussed in detail. The climax comes when it is claimed that they gain in four things — life, knowledge, fame and strength — of all such persons who salute and serve the old every day:

अभिवादनशीलस्य नित्यं वृद्धोपसेविनः।
चत्वारि तस्य वर्धन्ते आयुर्विद्या यशोबलम्।।

Abhivādansheelasya nityam bridhopasevinah
Chatwāri tasya vardhante āyurvidyā yasho balam

Father, mother and teacher: In the second chapter from slokas 225 to 235, *Manusmriti* deals with the honest service to be rendered to the elders particularly to father, mother and guru. It is essential for all to devote all their attention to these three sacred figures. If they follow this religion, they need not follow any other, because the father is like the God, the mother is like the Earth and brothers are the replicas of the self. The debts of the immediate creators — father and mother, cannot be repaid even after hundred years of selfless service. These three (parents and guru) are like three *āshrams* (phases of life), *trilok* (three worlds), *triveda* (three Vedas), and three *agnis* (father *gārhpatyāgni* or domestic fire, mother *dakshināgni* or southern fire, and the guru *āhwaneeyagni* or the fire of rituals). A person wins this world with his devotion to the mother, he wins Space with his devotion to father and the *Brahmaloka* with his devotion to his guru:

आचार्यश्च पिता चैव माता भ्राता च पूर्वजः।
नार्तेनाप्यवमन्तव्या ब्राह्मणेन विशेषतः।।

Āchāryascha pitā chaiva matā bhrātā cha purbajah
Nārtenāpyavamantvyā brāhmanena visheshtah

— *Manusmriti* (2:225)

आचार्यो ब्रह्मणो मूर्तिः पिता मूर्तिः प्रजापतेः।
माता पृथिव्या मूर्तिस्तु भ्राता स्वो मूर्तिरात्मनः।।

Āchāryo Brahmanomurtih pitā murtih prajāpateh
Mātā prithivyā murtiastu bhrātā swo murtih ātmanah

— *Manusmriti* (2:226)

तेषां त्रयाणां शुश्रूषा परमं तपः उच्यते।
न तैरभ्यननुज्ञातो धर्ममन्यं समाचरेत्।

Teshām trāyānām shushrushā paramam tapah uchayate Na tairabhyananugyāto dharmamanyam samāchareta

— *Manusmriti* (2:229)

Acceptance of essence: One must accept the essence, take knowledge and wisdom or an important art from those also who are low in caste or belong to the scheduled caste. The nectar should be taken off even from the poison, a good lesson from a child, a moral lesson from an enemy, and gold from even an impure place. In the same manner women, jewels, knowledge, religion, purity, proverbial teaching, and different types of art should be taken and accepted from any place. It makes no difference from where are such great and essential elements coming. *The essence is important, not the person, place or thing from which or where they are coming.*

Varnāshram (the division of society): Broadly speaking there are still only four classes in the society — the worker, the business community — the government machinery and the teachers, writers, engineers and scientists.

The communists accept only two communities — the worker and the owner. They forget the biggest, the most active and powerful middle class.

The Europeans have accepted only three — the high, low and middle class. Their fallacy is that they further divide each class in the same three classes on the similar pattern as the high middle class, middle class and lower middle class. Their classes are based only on the ground of material possession, wealth and modern living conditions. They do not think of the independent and personal growth of an individual which is essential because *man is at last judged by his inner possession, intellectual development, spiritual height and character.*

Manusmriti discusses the last and lasting effects of bad deeds when the immediate gains encourage the evil doer who is completely destroyed before his final tragic end. On the contrary, it praises the late but lasting gains of those who do only good to all.

अधर्मेणैधते तावत् ततो भद्राणि पश्यन्ति।
ततः सपत्रंजयति समूलस्तु विनश्यति।।

Adharmenaidhate tāwat tato bhadrāni pashyanti
Tatah sapatrānjayati samoolastu vinasayati

— *Manusmriti* (4:174)

(*Man first collects wealth through bad ways, then performs wholesome deeds, after that one is destroyed with leaves and roots.*)

One must read the book well and complete it first, only then one should say something for or against. A cursory glance or a partial truth cannot establish or refute the whole.

2. Yãgyavalkya Smriti

The second most important Hindu scripture is *Yãgyavalkya Smriti*. *Manusmriti* is accepted as the oldest one but *Yãgyavalkya Smriti* is equal in status, fame, purity and wisdom. Yãgyavalkya was the Guru of King Janak. His sacrifice, devotion and high moral standard impressed the Indian masses to such an extent that the spiritual, religious, social, political and moral standards established by him are treated as the most authentic and accepted by all.

Yãgyavalkya was a great visionary, balanced thinker and prolific writer. He is with reverence called Yogishwar Yãgyavalkya. He has written the following books:

1. *Yãgyavalkya Smriti*
2. *Brahmokta Yogia Yãgyavalkya Smriti*
3. *Brihad Yogia Yãgyavalkya Smriti*
4. *Yãgyavalkya Gitã*
5. *Yãgyavalkya Upanishad*
6. *Yãgyavalkya Shikshã*
7. *Yãgyavalkya Gãyatri Bhãshya*

There are many commentaries and explanatory books on the *Smritis* of Yãgyavalkya. The foremost among them are:

1. *Bãlbodhini*
2. *Bãlkrira* by Viswaroopa

3. *Subodhani*
4. *Bālambhatti*
5. *Deepakalika* by Achārya Shoolpāni
6. *Uprārka Vyākhyā* by Uoarāditya
7. *Mitāksharā* by Vigyāneshwar

Once in Mithila, the *rishis* requested him to explain and elucidate the religion and the religious activities of a human being. Whatever Maharshi Yāgyavalkya taught them was collected and came to be known as Yāgyavalkya Smriti. Around one thousand *slokas* have been divided into three chapters — a. *Āchār* b. *Vyawahār* and c. *Prayāschit*, on the pattern of *Manusmriti*.

The **first** chapter comprises:

1. Introduction (*Upodghāt*)
2. Celibacy (*Brahmacharya*)
3. Marriage (*Vivah*)
4. Caste-discretion (*Varnajātivivek*)
5. The duties of a householder (*Grihasthadharma*)
6. The duties of a bachelor (*Snātakdharma*)
7. Eatables and non-eatables (*Bhakshyabhakshya*)
8. Metal purification (*Dravyāshuddhi*)
9. Donation (*Dān*)
10. Last rites (*Shrāddha*)

11. The epoch of Ganesha (*Ganpatikalp*)
12. Pacification of planets (*Grihashānti*)
13. The duties of a king (*Rājdharma*)

The **second** chapter deals with the general behaviour and includes the following 25 topics:

1. General behaviour or duties of a mother (*Sādhāran vyavhār mātrikā*)
2. Special behaviour or duties of a mother (*Vishesh vyavhār mātrikā*)
3. Loans (*Rinadān*)
4. Subsidiary wealth (*Upnidhi*)
5. Witness (*Sākshi*)
6. Fit to be written (*Lekhya*)
7. Divine (*Divya*)
8. Debt (*Dāyabibhāg*)
9. Boundary in dispute (*Seemāvivād*)
10. Employee (*Swāmipālvivād*)
11. Sale deeds (*Swāmivikraya*)
12. Assignment (*Dattāpradānika*)
13. Purchase (*Kritānushaya*)
14. Preferential treatment (*Abhyupetyāshushrushā*)
15. Sensible default (*Sambidvytikram*)
16. Salary payment (*Vetandān*)

17. Gambling commands (*Dyutasamāhwaya*)
18. Eloquence (*Vākyapārushya*)
19. Punishing power (*Dandapārushya*)
20. Courage (*Sāhas*)
21. Equal distribution (*Vikriyāsampradān*)
22. Equal prosperity (*Sambhuyasamutthān*)
23. Burglary (*Asteya*)
24. Women collection (*Strisangrahan*)
25. Conclusion (*Prakirnak*)

The **third** chapter deals with expiation and includes the following six topics:

1. Purification (*Ashauch*)
2. Duties during emergency (*Apaddharma*)
3. The third stage in life (*Vānprastha*)
4. Asceticism (*Yatidharma*)
5. Expiation (*Prāyaschita*)
6. Conclusive expiation (*Prakirnak prāyaschita*)

Yāgyavalkya had many things to advise to all the human beings irrespective of the social or other divisions. The religious actions common to all the human beings was non-violence. He advised everyone to stop physical and oral violence and not even to think of violence. He asked each one to be truthful. One should never steal a thing. He considered both inner and outer cleanliness or purification and control over the senses as the most essential aspects of a religious life. One must donate something according to his ability. One must show control over his inner feelings, exhibit compassion towards all and should refrain from anger at heart, in words or in action:

अहिंसा सत्यमस्तेयंशौचमिन्द्रियनिग्रहः।
दानं दमो दया शांतिः सर्वेषां धर्मसाधनम्।।

Ahimsa satyamasteyam shauchamindriyanigrahah
Dānam damo dayā kshāntih sarvesām harmasādhanam

He advised all to be religious and to adopt religious ways and means, and to stop all malpractices. One should not do any such thing which is harmful to the society, is against life or is destructive in nature and effect.

कर्मणा मनसा वाचा यत्रधर्मं समाचरेत्।
अस्वर्गं लोकविद्विस्तं धर्म्यमव्याचरेन्न तु।।

Karmanā mansā vāchā yatradharmam samācharet
Aswargam lokvidwistam dharmyampyācharenna tu

(*Because the religious deeds increase longevity, grant noble children, wealth, knowledge, happiness, a place where one can rule, heaven and salvation, hence one must be religious and do only wholesome deeds.*)

अयं तु परमो धर्मो यद्योगेनात्मदर्शनम्।

Ayam tu parmo dharmo yadwogenātmadarshanam

(*According to Yāgyavalkya, self-revelation is the extreme end of religion which is possible only through yoga or union.*)

3. Vyās Smriti

The greatest of all human minds, Ved Vyās is the most revered figure among the *rishis*. He had the brightest halo behind his head and a series of great creations to his credit. He had all the knowledge in his mind. He edited them and arranged them meticulously well.

He was a complete 'Cosmic University' in himself. He was acclaimed to be one of the eight persons who never did depart from the earth.

Ved Vyās was the great grandson of Maharshi Vashishtha, grandson of Shakti Rishi, the son of Pārāsher and the father of Shukadeva on the one hand and that of Dhritrashtra, Pandu and Vidur on the other. Ved Vyās was not his real name. He was born in an island-like area in Yamuna region so he was given a name *'Dwaipāyan'*. Since he was dark in complexion, he was called *Krishnadwaipāyan*. He gave an exquisite order to Vedas, so he is known as Ved Vyās. It is said that different congregations of *rishis*, *munis* and *tapaswis* remained ceaselessly in session in his *āshram* where each one freely expressed whatever one had accumulated as his knowledge. One thing is clear that he did an outstanding job by collecting and classifying all the knowledge which is the basis of all human knowledge. Though *Mahābhārata* is an epic but it is almost a religious book, a scripture in the form of stories and incidents. One can call it an applied scripture. His two other works *Vyās Smriti* and *Laghuvyās Smriti* are regarded as the touchstones as they have special places among the scriptures known as *Smritis*.

The *Vyās Smriti* contains 250 *slokas* recited at Varanasi and divided into 4 chapters. The original book may have more *slokas* but only 250 are available. Primarily it deals with the types of places which can be worth living and where religion can grow. Every place is not fertile for the emergence and growth of a religion. It gives preference to Vedic Knowledge over everything and discusses sixteen methods and rituals to be adopted for becoming cultured and refined. The rules of celibacy and the greatness of gurus, marriage, including the characteristics of a marriageable girl, have been neatly presented in the most concise form. With the same precision and dexterity he has dealt with the daily, occasional and desired duties of a householder and a woman's daily duties, her duties towards her husband and household during her mestrual cycle. He has praised the household, moral living and Brahmins. The last 50 *slokas* deal with the offerings (donations), so it is often called *Dān Smriti.* One can be baptised into the following 16 different ways at different stages of life for different gains. They are:

गर्भाधानं पुंसवनं सीमन्तो जातकर्म च।
नामक्रिया निष्क्रमणेन्नाशनं वपनक्रिया।।

कर्णवेधो व्रतादेशो वेदारम्भ क्रियाविधिः।
केशान्तः स्नानमुद्वाहो विवाहाग्नि परिग्रहः।।
त्रेताग्नि संग्रहश्चेति संस्काराः षोडश स्मृताः।

Garbhādhānam punsvanam seemānto jātkarma cha
Nāmkriyā niskramaneannāsam vapankriyā
Karnbedho vratādesho vedārambha kriāvidhih
Keshāntah snānmudwāho vivāhagni parigrahah
Tretāgni sangrahscheti samskārāh shodas smritāh

—*Vyās Smriti* (1:13-15)

1. Conception (*garbhādhānam*), for better children
2. Fertilisation (*punswan*), three months after conception for 'life-being' and safety
3. Upgradation of limitations (*seemantoannayan*), a month before delivery for safe and secure birth
4. The ceremony performed just after the birth of a child (*jātkarma*), to be sure that all necessary precautions have been taken
5. Naming (*nāmakaran*), eleven days after the birth to give an individual identity
6. Ceremoniously going out (*niskraman*), after four months the child is taken out into the open to face the wind and sunshine
7. Ceremoniously giving a child its first cereal food (*annaprāshana*) after six months

8. Sowing seeds (*vapankriyā*)
9. Investiture with the sacred thread (*upnayan*)
10. Piercing of ears (*karnabedha*)
11. Offering of hair (*keshant/shamshru*)
12. Initiation into study (*vedārambh*), to start study
13. Convocation or Baptism into Vedas (*vedasnān*)
14. Marriage (*vivāh*)
15. Encircling the marriage-fire (*vivāhgniparigrah*)
16. Baptism into the conservation of fire (*tretāgnisangrah*) to start a domestic life

In the *Dān Smriti*, Vyās laid stress that in the *'Kaliyug'*, the running epoch, offering or donation is the only saviour: *dānmekam kalaujuge.*

The acquisition of religious deeds is the greatest wealth for everything else will perish but the religious deeds will outlive all: *dharmādartho bhawedadhruvam.*

The ***Laghu Vyās Smriti*** laid ample stress on early rising, cleanliness, freedom from defilement, bathing, water-offering, evening prayer, offering water to the sun for remaining free from blood pressure, heart disease and skin disease, recitation of *Gāyatri Mantra*, servitude to guests and sound sleep, etc. He advocated seven types of bathing to suit the needs of all from a patient to a labourer. Those who fail to perform the evening prayer remain vile all the time. The things done without the evening prayer never bear expected results:

तस्मात् सर्वप्रयत्नेन संध्योपासं समाचरेत्।
उपासितो भवेत् तेन देवयोगतनुः प्रकाशयेत्।।

Tasmāt sarvaprayatanen sandhyopāsam samācharet
Upāsito bhawet tena devyogatanuh prakāshayet

— *Laghu Vyās Smriti* (1:30)

One must feed the animals, guests and the servants first. One should take food only after feeding them:

अभ्यागतान् यथाशक्ति भोजदेयदतिथिं सदा।
अदत्त्वा देवताभूतभृत्यातिथि पितृष्वपि।।
भुंजीत चेत् स मूढ़ात्मा तिर्यग्योनिं च गच्छति।

Abhyāgatān yathāshakti bhojdeydatithim sadā
Adatwā devatābhutabhrityā tithi pitriswapi
Bhunjeet cheta sa mudhātmā tiryagyonim cha gachchhati

— *Laghu Vyās Smriti* (2:62-63)

4. Bhagwān Vishnu Smriti or Vishnu Dharmasutra

It is a very interesting and absorbing mythical legend. The time set is just after the incarnation of Vishnu as *'Vārāhāwatār'* when he got the earth from the bottom of the sea. The earth had come out of the sea but had no axis to stand and no fixed route to rotate or revolve. She was drifting aimlessly. Earth went to her father Maharshi Kashyap (The earth is deemed to be the daughter or the creation of Maharshi Kashyap and is known as Kashyapi also) and narrated her woe. He suggested her to go to Vishnu for more knowledge and further direction. She went to Lord Vishnu and said, "O God of Gods, I had fallen deep into the sea. You granted me salvation, but I have no base to stand. Please tell me who will hold me in the space and stop me from falling again." Lord Vishnu said, "The whole Cosmos is based on *dharma* (religion) which is held by religious people, saints, sages and pious souls. Only they will save you, hold you, keep you intact, complete, alive and active. They know the pure religion. They follow religion, so they are all powerful and capable to hold you."

वर्णाश्रमाचाररता: शास्त्रैकतत्परायणा:।
त्वां धरे धारयिष्यन्ति तेषां तखार आहित:।।

Varnāshramāchāraratah shāstraiktatparāyanāh
Twām dhare dhārishyanti teshām tadbhār āhitah

The earth was happy to listen to the encouraging statement of the Lord. She further requested him to disclose the secret of the 'religion'. In response to her request whatever Lord Vishnu said to earth is known as ***Vishnu Smriti*** or ***Vishnu Sutra***. It is in the form of dialogue between the Lord and the earth.

There are exactly 100 chapters in *Vishnu Smriti*. It has been said in maxims or percepts. It is said to be an integral part of the Katha Branch of scriptures. Many *slokas* from *Manusmriti*, the *Gita*, *Garuda Purāna* and *Yoga* have been quoted in their original form. It is the principal book of *Vaishnava Dharma* and was meticulously and honestly followed by Ramãnujãchãrya, Madhavãchãrya, Nimbãrkãchãrya, Ballabhãchãrya, Vishnuswãmi and Ramãnand, and their countless followers.

All the general teachings for purification and growth is the same as taught in other *Smritis*. As for example:

क्षमा सत्यं दमः शौचं दानमिन्द्रियसंयमः।
अहिंसा गुरुशुश्रूषा तीर्थानुसरणं दया।।

Chhamã satyam damah shaucham dãnamindriysanyamah
Ahimsa gurushushrushã teerthãnusharanam dayã

आर्जवत्वमलोभश्च देवब्राह्मणपूजनम्।
अनभ्यसूया च यथा धर्मः समान्य उच्यते।

Arjavatwamlobhascha devbrahmana poojanam
Anabhyasuyã cha yathã dharamah sãmãnya uchyate

The king should see whether the people are honestly doing their respective duties or not. He must ensure organised and sincere effort:

प्रजापरिपालनं वर्णाश्रमाणां स्वे-स्वे धर्मे व्यवस्थापनम्।

Prajãparipãlanam varnãshramãnãm swe swe dharme vyawasthãpanam

The king is responsible for the 1/6th part of the sins and crimes committed by his people as he takes that much share in their good deeds:

राजा च प्रजाभ्यः सुकृतदुष्कृतषष्ठांशभाक्।

Rãjã cha prajabhyah sukritduskritshashatãnshbhãk

In *Vishnu Smriti*, time is taken as infinite and omnipotent. It claims the system of change to be changeless. It says that in different epochs, different Indrãs, Devtãs and Manus appear and disappear. Man has no say in it. Those who are born in the world will die. Only religion and religious deeds can save from acute or excessive pain and suffering:

जातस्य ही ध्रुवोमृत्यु ध्रुवं जन्ममृतस्य च।
अर्थे दुष्परिहार्येऽस्मिन नास्ति लोके सहायक:।।

Jãtasya hi dhruvomrityu dhruvam janmamritasya cha
Arthe dusparibaryeyasmin nãsti loke sahãyakah

As a calf recognises correctly and reaches its mother among thousands of cows, in the same manner the deeds of men come to them in their every life. Moral acts and ideal deeds add to health, life, pleasure and prosperity while immoral acts and bad deeds destroy them completely.

There is another very revealing exchange of dialogues in the form of questions and answers. Earth saw Lakshmi with Vishnu. She was lured to ask some questions and get answers directly from her. So she asked her, "Where do you reside other than the Lord?" Lakshmi smiled and in well-rehearsed and well-modulated words, she declared all her abodes. She said that she resides in young horse, ox and studious Brãhmin, in cow-milk, honey and green fertile land, young maiden, *devatãs*, *tapaswis* and in the organisers of *yajna*. She further added that she resides in white flowers, hills and mountains, fruits, fascinating rivers, clean lakes and ponds and in lotus.

She said that she resides in children, saints, religious persons, forests, calves, pious persons and in such persons who have control over their senses. She claimed to live in truthful, compassionate and kind persons and also in those who have forebearance, tolerance, faith and are skilled in their work.

Lakshmi revealed a secret that she resides in housewives provided that they are honest to their husbands and softspoken:

Pativratāsu priyavādinisu.

She further added that she lives in kind and religious ladies. Though the list of the different abodes of Lakshmi given here is not complete but it definitely shows her preferences and give us an insight to decide as to what should we do for attracting Goddess Lakshmi to live as close to us as possible.

Vishnu Smriti divides ascetics into four kinds. They are:

1. **Kutichak,** who has renunciated all and has no inclination and lives by begging
2. **Bahudaka,** who lives like the first one, recites *Gāyatri Mantra* and meditates over the Universal God after controlling the sense organs and sensual feelings
3. **Hans,** who has renunciated his family, has control over the senses and tries for salvation through penance
4. **Paramhans** is the one who is said to be *dhyānbhikshu* (eager for meditation) and aims at the union with the

Absolute *Brahman*. He leads a self-centred inner life after renunciating everything. He wears only a *kaupin* (a small piece of cloth) and a shawl and keeps a *danda* (a special thick, small staff). He has no anger, no lust and is fully humble.

5. Parăsher Smriti

Maharshi Parăsher was the father of Ved Vyăs. He was the grandson of Maharshi Vashishtha and the son of Mahătma Shakti. In this way, he is the grandfather of Sri Shukdev Muni. He compiled an easy sripture based on the general and prosperous life which was simple enough for all the persons to follow. It is to be followed in the modern *Kaliyug* as *Manusmriti* was adopted in *Satyug*, Gautam's scripture in *Tretăyug* and Shankh's *Smriti* during *Dwăparyug*:

कृते तु मानवो धर्मस्त्रैतायाम गौतमः स्मृतः।
द्वापरे शंखलिखितः कलौ पराशरः स्मृतः।।

Krite tu mănawo dharmastretăyăm Gautamah smritah
Dwapare Shankhalikhitah Kalau Parăsherah smritah

— *Parăsher* (1:24)

Both the *Laghu* and *Brihad Parăsher Smritis* have 12 chapters each but the latter has many other *slokas* than the former one. Cows and Brahmins have been well adulated in it. He who sacrifices his everything and even his life to protect a cow or a Brahmin is freed from the most heinous sins like *brāhmhatya* (killing of a Brāhmin):

ब्राह्मणार्थे गवार्थे वा यस्तु प्राणान् परित्यजे।
मुच्यते ब्रह्महत्याद्वैगोरप्ता गोब्राह्मणस्य च।।

Brāhmanārthe gawārthe wā yastu prānān parityaje
Muchyate brahmahatyādwaigorptā gobrāhmanasya cha

— *Parāsher* (8:42)

Parāsher treats abortion to be the worst crime, the most heinous one, a greater sin than the killing of a Brāhmin:

यत्पापं ब्रह्महत्याया द्विगुणं गर्भपातने।
प्रायश्चितं न तस्यास्ति तस्यास्त्यागो विधियते।

Yatpāpam brahmahatyāyā dwigunam garbhapātane
Prāyaschitam na tasyasti tasyāstyāgo bidhiyate

— *Parāsher* (4:20)

Parāsher pointed out that such a child who dies just after birth or before its teeth come out should not be put to ritual pyre for cremation.

Only religious activities can ensure the welfare of the mankind. One psychological behaviour that Parāsher stressed is that one should not do what one dislikes. If one abuses an act and himself indulges into it, he becomes a laughing stock. He neither grows nor is believed:

परेषां यदसूयेत न तत् कुर्यात् स्वयं नरः।
यो ह्यसूयुस्तथायुक्तः सोऽवहासं नियच्छति।।

Pareshām yadsuyeta na tat kuryāt swayam narah
Yo hyasuyustathāyuktah soawāhāsam niyachchhati

— *Shānti Parva, Mahābhārata*

So it is always better to follow the scriptures and to perform only such acts which are respected as religious. One must keep distance from sinful deeds:

धर्म एव कृत: श्रेयानिहलोके परत्र च।
तस्माद्धि परमं नास्ति यथा प्राहुर्मनीषण:।।

Dharma yewa kritah shreyānihloke paratra cha
Tasmāddhi paramam nāsti yathā prāhurmanishanah

— *Shānti Parva, Mahābhārata*

So it is essential to remain in close contact with only religious persons and always stay away from criminals and sinners:

सखिस्तु सह संसर्ग:शोभते धर्मदर्शिभि:।
नित्यं सर्वास्ववस्थासु नासखिरिति मे मति:।।

Sadbhistu sah sansargah shobhate dharmadarshibhih
Nityam sarvāswaawasthāsu nāsdibhiriti me matih

— *Shānti Parva, Mahābhārata*

The wealth earned through immoral means and criminal deeds is self-destructive in nature. The wealth accumulated through rightful and religious means is the real wealth which helps one to grow and keeps one healthy and happy:

येऽर्था धर्मेण ते सत्या येऽधर्मेण धिगस्तुतान्।
धर्मं वै शाश्वतं लोके न जह्याद धनाकांक्षया।।

Ye arthā dharmena te satyā yeadharmena dhigastutān
Dharmam wai shāswatam loke na jahyād dhanākānkshayā

— *Shānti Parva, Mahābhārata*

A man must keep four things in mind for peace:

तस्मात् प्रकाशयेत पापं स्वधर्मं सततं चरेत्।
स्त्रीबालभृत्यगोविप्रेष्वतिकोपं विवर्जयेत्।।

Tasmāt prakāshayet pāpam swadharmam satatam charet
Stribālbhrityagovipreshwatikopam vivarjayet

— *Parāsher* (9:62)

i. He should clearly declare his irreligious activities and sins already committed.
ii. He should refrain from committing sins.
iii. He should always follow his own religion.
iv. He should never show anger to women, children, servants, patients and to one who is aggrieved.

Parāsher gave a lot of importance to cows and found it to be the only way to get rid of the sins, to get peace and prosperity. He held the view that all the gods reside in the different parts of a cow. One who feels like that and shows no anger towards cows and serves them well, gets prosperity in this world and goes to heaven after death:

एवं यो वर्तते गोषु ताऽनक्रोधवर्जितः।
महतीं श्रियमाप्नोति स्वर्गलोके महीयते।।

Yewam yo vartate goshu tãnkrodhvarjitah
Mahatim shriyamãpnoti swargaloke mahiyate

— *Parãsher* (5:41)

If one treats the cows as the greatest wealth, salutes them, moves round them, then he can be assured of peace and prosperity. A round taken of a cow is like the round taken of the whole earth with seven seas:

संस्पृशन् गां नमस्कृत्य कुर्यात् तां च प्रदक्षिणम्।
प्रदक्षिणीकृता तेन सप्तद्वीपा वसुन्धरा।।

Sansprishan gãm namaskritya kuryãt tãm pradakshinam
Pradakshinikritã tena saptadweepã vasundhara

— *Parãsher* (5:541)

6. Aitareya Smriti

Maharshi Atri is one of the seven *rishis* known as the constellation *Saptrishi* or Ursã Major in northern sky. He is the husband of Mahãsati Anusuyã who is herself well known for her purity and divinity and many divine deeds.

His Scriptures are known as *Aitareya Smriti* and *Aitareya Samhitã*. The 90 *slokas* of the former are divided in nine chapters.

Maharshi Atri advised all to show respect and study the Vedas but he clearly stated that one should not ignore the scriptures. If one ignores them, he will have to take birth as an animal in his next life:

वेदं गृहीत्वा यः कश्चिच्छास्त्रं चैवावमन्यते।
स सद्यः पशुतां याति सम्भावनेकविंशतिम्।।

Vedam gribitwa yah kaschichchhāstram chaivāvamanyate
Sa sadyah pashutām yāti sambhāwanekavinshatim

— *Aitareya Samhita*

Atri claimed that the householder who possessed all the eight characteristics of an ideal householder became pure as a Brāhmin, got elevated in life and was freed from the endless cycle of birth, death and rebirth:

यश्चैतैर्लक्षणयुक्तो गृहस्थोऽपि भवेद द्विजः।
स गच्छति परं स्थानं जायते नेह वै पुनः।।

Yaschaitairlakshanyukto gribastoapi bhaweda dwijah
Sa gachchhati param sthānam jāyate neh wai punah

— *Aitareya Samhitā* (42)

Now, there can be a simple question as to what are those eight characteristics of such an ideal householder. Atri discussed them in detail in the *Aitareya Samhitā* from *slokas* 34 to 41. They are:

i. *Anusuyā* or to see and praise only the good qualities of a man
ii. *Shauch* which usually means purity but it also includes not to eat non-eatables, not to be associated with bad characters, to think in a healthy way and to perform only moral acts

iii. *Mangal* is to follow good path and get associated with good people

iv. *Anāyās* or not to perform such tasks which give pain to body or add to ill-health, and to do only such works which are easier to perform and suitable to the body

v. *Asprihā* or to be satisfied with the lady married to him and not be lured by better women

vi. *Dama* or the ability to remain calm and cool even when instigated or victimised by others

vii. *Dān* or to give something in charity out of the daily earning

viii. *Dayā* or kindness, sympathy and compassion

The most interesting aspect of *Aitareya Smriti* is the declaration about the sinners. What one is facing in this life is the result of the sins committed in the previous life, and the crimes and sins that one commits in this life show the same result in the next life. So Atri advised all to lead a clean and pure life. He said if a man, who has everything and does only wholesome deeds, is yet suffering, then it must be the effect of the things done during his last life. Atri has very clearly stated the results which are as follows:

1. *Nyasapahāri chānpatyah* – He gets no children who steals from a trust-fund.

2. *Ratnāpahāri chātyanta daridrah* – A jewel thief lives in penurious condition.
3. *Devalasharnātchāndālah* – He becomes a sinful untouchable burning-*ghāt* keeper who steals from a temple or such pious places.
4. *Itastatastarkako mārjārah* – An atheist and one who is illogical and vociferous becomes a he-cat.
5. *Kakchhāgārdāhak khadyota* – He who sets houses on fire, is born as a firefly.
6. *Dhānyaharanānmushakah* – He who steals cereals takes birth as a rat in rotund family.
7. *Bhritakādhyāpakah shrigālah* – The teacher who takes money for teaching becomes a jackal.
8. *Pardravyaharnāt pretah* – He becomes a ghost who steals money.
9. *Sarvadāhanritavachanāt pāpah* – He is the greatest sinner who always keeps on telling lies.
10. *Vārdhushikah kurmah* – A profiteer is born as tortoise.
11. *Urnanābho nāstikah kritaghnascha* – Atheists and ungrateful people are born as spiders.
12. *Sharanāgatatyāgi brahmarākshah* – He becomes a demonic gnome who refuses to give shelter to one who requests for the same.

7. Vashishtha Smriti

With his compassionate and tolerant nature, Maharshi Vashishtha became the most honoured *rishi* among those great intellectual and spiritual beings. His nature, character and contributions are the most quoted and discussed things in and about the divine Vedic literature. His life, words and contributions have been mentioned in most of the books.

According to the *Purānas,* Vashishtha was born out of the mind of *Brahman* but according to the Vedas he was the son of Mitrāvarun. He envisioned the Vedic *mantras* which have been collected in the seventh mandal of the *Rig Veda* which is dedicated to and known by his name. He was the most revered *rishi* among the constellation of *Saptarishis* or Ursā Major. A very honoured lady Devi Arundhati was his wife who was never separated from him and is still seen in the sky as a bright star. They are both worshipped for a long, happy and prosperous conjugal life.

Other than the Vedic *mantras*, and things mentioned above Maharshi Vashishtha is known for many more things:

- He was the grandfather of Maharshi Ved Vyās and great grandfather of Shukdev Muni.
- He was the famous Guru of *Raghukula* and Rama.
- He wrote the divine book *Yoga Vashishtha.*
- He gave the world two illuminating treatises

named *Vashishtha Dharmasutra* and *Vashishtha Smriti.*

- He opposed Vishwāmitra and bore his anger with patience and tolerance.
- Vashishtha and Arundhati served the cows and possessed one special cow, the daughter of Kāmdhenu named Nandini.
- He, along with his wife Arundhati, dedicated his whole life to humanity.

Vashishtha was very clear about the religious and irreligious deeds and duties. All his revealing and regulatory Sutras have been collected in two books known as ***Vashishtha Dharmasutra*** (VD) and ***Vashishtha Smriti.***

Vashishtha claimed that whatever is given in the Shrutis and Smritis is Religion: ***Shrutismritivihito dharmah*** (VD 1:3) and if in such cases where proofs are not found then one should follow the saints, sages and other great men: ***Tadlābhe shishtāchārah pramānam*** (VD 1:4). He defines the gentry as such civilised and cultured men who have sacrificed everything: ***Shishtah punarakāmātmā*** (VD 1:5). He advised all to know and follow religion.

One thing that one is unable to understand is his strong attitude against the evildoers. He himself did not punish Vishwāmitra but he said that it was not a sin to kill a treacherous person:

आततायिनं हत्वा नात्र प्राणच्छेतुः किंचित् किल्विषमाहुः।

Atatāyeenam hatwa nātra prānchchhetuh kinchita kilvisamāhu

— *Vashishtha Dharmasutra* (3:16)

In his eyes there are six types of such treacherous persons: one who sets something ablaze, one who administers poison, one who kills with arms in hand, one who forcibly takes away wealth or land or women:

अग्निदो गरदश्चैव शस्त्रपाणिर्धनापहः।
क्षेत्रदार हरश्चैव षडेते ह्याततायिनः।।

Agnido garadaschaiva shastrapānirdhanāpahah
Kshetradārharaschaiva shadete hyātatāyinah

— *Vashishtha Dharmasutra* (3:19)

For the emancipation, he clearly states that mind is purified with knowledge, body is purified after taking a bath with clean water, the purgation of heart is achieved by following truth, and religion and life is purified with penance:

अखिर्गात्राणि शुध्यन्ति मनः सत्येन शुध्यति।
विद्यातपोभ्यां भूतात्मा बुद्धिर्ज्ञानेन शुध्यति।।

Adbhirgātrāni shudhyanti manah satyen shudhayati
Vidyātapobhyām bhutātmā buddhirgyānen shudhyati

—*Vashishtha Dharmasutra* (3:56)

Vashishtha said that the soil from the five following five places should not be used in rituals because it is impure:

a) from inside water

b) from a temple

c) from an ant-hill

d) collected by rat

e) leftover after cleaning hand

अन्तर्जले देवगृहे वल्मीके मूषकस्थले।
कृतशौचावशिष्टा च न ग्राह्याः पंच मृत्तिकाः।।

Antarjale devagrihe valmike mushaksthale
Kritshauchāvashishtā cha na grāhyāh panch mritikāh

— *Vashishtha Dharmasutra* (6:15)

According to Vashishtha, lust is the basic reason behind pain, suffering and immoral activities. One's lust is never satiated. On the contrary, it incessantly grows. Once a man falls in the hardened grip of lust, he cannot be free even when he is completely ruined. So, one must not encourage lust and must lead a life of frugality and contentment. The moment one opts for extravagance, he takes the ruinous path of crime, falsehood and immoral activities. He should feel satisfied with the religious deeds:

जीर्यन्ति जीर्यतः केशा दन्ता जीर्यन्ति जीर्यतः।
जीवनाशा धननाशा च जीर्यतोऽपि न जीर्यति।।
या दुस्त्यजा दुर्मतिभिर्या न जीर्यते जीर्यतः।
योऽसौ प्राणान्तिको रोगस्तां तृष्णां त्यजतः सुखम।।

Jeerayanti jeerayatah keshā dantā jeerayanti jeerayatah
Jivanāshā dhananāshā cha jeerayatoapi na jeerayati
Yā dustyajā durmatibhiryā na jeerayati jeerayatah
Yoasou prānāntiko rogastām trishnām tyajatah sukham

— *Vashishtha Dharmasutra* (3:10-11)

Vashishtha Smriti also contains great teachings for better growth and happier life. It contains 1150 *slokas* which have been divided into 7 chapters. It is an answer to the enquiries by Ved Vyās and other *rishis*. It created a tradition and the *Smritis* that followed adopted the concept of Maharshi Vashishtha. Naturally most of the chapters deal with the general subjets of the duties of the kings and the people of all the four social divisions. The most important teaching for the women comes in the fifth chapter. The modern women who are trying hard to compete with men in general work are fast losing womanhood. They are unable to get adequate mental satisfaction. They are now the most dissatisfied lot. As a result, the family life is ruined because their sweetness, smoothness, gentleness, love and compassion is overpowered by manly feelings of financial success. Women are best known for and are capable of giving birth, fostering with care and changing a hut or a house into a cosy home for peace, pleasure and all-round development. Maharshi Vashishtha has a lot to say about them. To be sweet and gentle is the first quality of a woman:

शीलमेव तु नारीणां प्रधानं धर्म उच्यते।

Sheelmewa tu nārinām pradhān dharma uchyate

She is the most successful woman who accepts her husband as a friend, a master and god. She should never disobey him:

पतिर्हि देवतं नार्याः पतिर्बन्धुः पतिर्गतिः।
तस्याज्ञां लंघयित्वैव नारी नरकमब्रूयात्।

Patirhi daivatam nāryāh patirbandhuh patirgatih
Tasyāgyām langhayeetvaiva nāri narakamabruyāt

She should be satisfied with what she gets and satisfy the husband and other family members with right deeds. She should be religious and follow her husband. She should not use rough words. On the contrary, she should be honey-tongued. She should not feel aggrieved at anything. She should not disobey her husband even under troublesome moments and intense suffering:

संतोषं परमास्थाय पतिं संतोषयेद् गुणैः।
सदा धर्मपथे युक्ता सदा भर्तृपरायणा।।
परुषं न वदेत् किंचित् सदा मधुरवाग्भवेत्।
यथोत्पन्नेन द्रव्येण संतुष्टा विगतज्वरा।।
परमापद्गता वापि भर्तारं न निषेधयेत्।

Santosham parmāsthāya patim santoshyed gunaih
Sadā dharmpathe yuktā sadā bharitriparāyanā
Parusham na vadet kinchita sadā madhurvagbhawet
Yathotpannena dravyena santushthā bigatajwarā
Permāpadgatā wāpi bhartāram na nishedhayet

— *Vashishtha Smriti* (5:61-63)

8. Mārkandeya Smriti

या देवि सर्वभूतेषु विद्यारूपेण संस्थिता।
नमस्तस्यै नमस्तस्यै नमस्तस्यै नमोनमः।।

Yā devi sarbabhuteshu vidyārupen sansthitā
Namastasyai namastasyai namastasyai namonamah

Maharshi Mārkandeya prayed to Goddess Durgā in Sri Durgāsaptshati, "O Goddess! You are all. Live in me in the form of wisdom. For it, I thrice salute thee."

Maharshi Mārkandeya was so gentle and humble that he treated all with honour, showed respect towards all. He is widely known for many things: *Skand Purāna*, *Mārkandeya Purāna* and *Mārkandeya Smriti*, *Sri Durgāsaptshati*, *Rewākhand* and *Mrityunjay Strotra* (not the *Mahāmrityunjay jāp mantra*).

A stanza from the prayer for Lord of Lords, Devādhideva Mahādeva, which says that a person under the protection of Lord Shiva cannot be harmed by death, is quoted below. The rest of it is available in *Strotra Ratnāwali:*

रत्नसानुशरासनं रजताद्रि श्रृंगनिकेतनं
शिंजनीकृत पन्नगेश्वरम अच्युतानलसायकम्।
क्षिप्रदग्धपुरत्रयं त्रिदशालयैः अभिवन्दितं
चन्द्रशेखरमाश्रये मम किं करिष्यति वै यमः।।

Ratnasānusharāsanam rajatādrishringniketanam
Shinjanikritpannageswaram achyutānalsāyakam
Kshipradagdhapuratrayam tridashālaih abhibanditam
Chandrashekharamāshraye mam kim karishyati wai yamah

Maharshi Mārkandeya had achieved a lot while he was a *muni* and when he became a *rishi* he created many more things. There are many popular mythical tales that shed light on the life, nature, character, deeds and achievements of Maharshi Mārkandeya. He is worshipped for always remaining young. Particular *mantras* have been specially composed in his honour. He remained a young, strong and healthy 25-year-old man throughout his life. Old age did not dare touch his perfect youth. It is mentioned in the *Van Parva* (183:42-43) of the *Mahābhārata*:

अजरश्च अमरश्चैव रूपौदार्यगुणान्वित:।
व्यदृश्यत तथा युक्तो तथा स्यात् पंचविंशक:।

Ajarascha amaraschaiva rupoudāryagunāniwitah
Vyadrisyata tathā yukto yathā syāt panchvinshakah

The myths claim that it was all because of his humble nature and the salutations that he devotedly offered to each Brāhmin that he met. It is said that he was blessed by the *Saptarishis* who requested Brahmā to grant him ageless life. Brahmā was already pleased with this devotee. Brahmā made him immortal and free of old age. The myths also claim that the God himself showed this illusory creation to Mārkandeya. There is another myth which claims that he was worshipping Lord Shiva when Death came to take him away. Shiva appeared from that very *Shivaling* to save Mārkandeya and made him immortal.

These are the reasons how Mārkandeya was able to grasp the reality behind healthy, pleasant and ageless life. He taught them in detail. The essence of his teaching was that he who led **a truly pious life**, and becomes a living symbol of all the human qualities, got the best of all the three worlds, which could never be cut short for it is '*akshaya*'. All those who perform their duties honestly, sincerely and consciously go to heaven. Reading *Mārkandeya Smriti* well, cleanses the conscience and gives the confidence to be pious and to be able to move on the path of humanity under every threat because heavenly pleasure and bliss are endowed on such a person:

मातापितृपरा ये च गुरुभक्ताः प्रियंवदाः।
सत्यार्जवरता ये च ते नराः स्वर्गगामिनः।।
परोपकारसक्ताश्च परदारविवर्जिताः।
पूज्यपूजयितारश्च ते नराः स्वर्गगामिनः।।

Mātāpitriparā ye cha gurubhaktāh priyamvadāh
Styārjvaratā ye cha te narāh swargagāminah
Paropakārasaktāscha pardārvivarjitāh
Pujyapujayitārascha te narāh swargagāminah

Mārkandeya Smriti (117:18-19) should be read to understand as to from where the Indians get the tolerance and what is the philosophy and psychology behind their good wishes for both the friend and the foe:

इति मत्वा समस्तेषु भोलोकाः कृतबुद्धयः।
सन्तु मा लौकिकं पापं लोकान प्राप्स्यथ वैबुधाः।।

यो मेऽद्य स्निह्यते तस्य शिवमस्तु सदा भुवि।
यश्च मां द्वेष्टि लोकेऽस्मिन् सोऽपि भद्राणि पश्यतु।।

Iti matvā samasteshu bho lokāh kritabuddhayah
Santu mā laukikam pāpam lokān prāpyastha waibudhāh
Yo meyadya snihayate tasya shivamastu sadā bhuvi
Yascha mām dwesti lokeyasmin soapi bhadrāni pasyatu

— *Mārkandeya Smriti* (117:18-19)

Mārkandeya claimed that if a foolish person did bring even a bit of harm to someone, he was bound to get punished. So one must not think in terms of doing harm to anyone:

यत् करोत्यहितं किंचित् कस्यचिन्मूढमानसः।
तं समभ्येति तन्नूनं कर्तृगामि फलं यतः।।

Yat karotyahitam kinchit kasyachinmoodhmānasah
Tam sambhyeti tannunam kartrigāmi phalam yatah

— *Mārkandeya Smriti* (117:17)

9. Āpastamba Smriti

Āpastamba was one of the most ancient Vedic *rishi*. He was the principal *āchārya* of the *Krishna Yajur Veda*. Sage Pānini has mentioned him in *Vidādi ganasutra* (4:1:104). His descendents mostly live in South India. There are tales, mostly in *Matsya Purāna* that he used to go for meditation deep inside some water body. He was against violence of any sort towards any living being, particularly the healthy fish which brought no harm. He once declared, "It makes no difference whether I go to heaven or to hell, I must take on myself the pain and suffering of all these innocent creatures. I wish that peaceful and prosperous life be granted to the aggrieved creatures with all sacred virtues that I have accumulated with my pure mind, words and physical and mental actions, through all my pious deeds."

He gave all his virtues for their liberation from suffering:

नरकं यदि पश्यामि वत्स्यामि स्वर्ग एववा।
यन्मया सुकृतं किंचिन्मनोवाक्कायकर्मभिः।
कृतं तेनापि दुःखार्ता सर्वेयान्तु शुभांगतिम्।।

Narakam yadi pasyāmi vatsyāmi swarga yeva wā
Yanmayā sukritam kinchinmanowākkāyakarmabhih
Kritam tenāpi dukhārtāh sarve yāntu shubhām gatim

— *Skand Purāna, Rewā Khand* (13:77-78)

In place of having such compassionate and kind wishes for other creatures, we are recklessly killing and destroying all the living beings (including humans) and non-living things.

Āpastamba composed and compiled many treatises which are real human heritage. They are:

i. *Āpastamba Shroutsutra*
ii. *Āpastamba Dharmasutra*
iii. *Āpastamba Grihyasutra*

iv. *Āpastamb Shulvasutra*

v. *Āpastamba Yagyaparibhāshāsutra*

vi. *Āpastamba Smriti*

These are all parts of the scriptures but only *Āpastamba Dharmasutra* and *Āpastamba Smriti* will be discussed here in short. We must know the scriptures and follow the instructions and teachings for the better, happier and a more pleasant life. These scriptures are for all times. The 'immediate present' has wisely been excluded. Naturally, they become 'Eternal Scriptures'.

The observations and the judgements of Āpastamba were so authentic and natural, genuine and religious that most of the *Smritis* have quoted him by saying 'As Āpastamba says' (*Āpastamba vacho yathā*).

(i) ***Āpastamba Dharmasutra:*** *Āpastamba Dharmasutra* is composed of *sutras* which have been condensed to be the smallest in size but they cover a vast field with their meanings. Broadly speaking, it is divided into two questions. The first question has 11 chapters (*Patals*) and 32 corpuscles (*Kanikās*), the second question too has 11 chapters (*Patals*) but only 29 corpuscles (*Kanikās*). Āpastamba started his dissertation with the assertion that the life, deeds and ideals of pious men, great saints and ancient sages were authentic proofs of religious life and concept, hence they should also be followed apart from what is written in the scriptures.

अथातः सामयाचारिकान् धर्मान् व्याख्यास्यामः
धर्मज्ञसमयः प्रमाणम्।।

Athātah sāmayāchārikān dharmān vyākhyāshyāmah Dharmagyasamayah pramānam

Whatever pious persons accept and follow should be accepted and followed; while whatever they reject or denounce should be readily denounced and rejected.

यं त्वार्याः क्रियमाणं प्रशंसन्ति स धर्मो यं गर्हन्ते सोऽधर्मः।

Yam twāryāh kriyamānam prashansanti sa dharmo yam garhante soadharmah

— *Āpastamba Dharmasutra* (7:7)

Āpastamba defined and explained an *āchārya* or a teacher as:

He who gives 'a religious conduct' is a teacher. No one should think of revolting against him: ***Tasmai na druhyaet kadāchan*** (1:15). An *āchārya* first refines a pupil and changes him into a man, and then metamorphoses him into a sublime, divine and saintly figure, even better than the gods. Parents only give body and life, but the teacher gives knowledge, the analytical and synthesising capacity and makes the pupil grow from inside. It is the second birth into Brahminhood:

स हि विद्यातस्तं जनयति।।
तच्छ्रेष्ठं जन्मः।।
शरीरमेव मातापितरौ जनयतः।।

Sa hi vidyātastam janyati
Tatshreshtham janamah
Shareeramewa mātāpitarau janayatah

— *Āpastamba Dharmasutra* (1:16-18)

Āpastamba has suggested all, never to go astray and one should not break relation with human deeds. They give all both directly and indirectly. He cites the example of a mango tree. We plant a mango tree for its juicy, sweet fruit which is full of pulp. When the tree bears the fruit we get fruit as well as shade, wood, leaves, smell and it purifies the atmosphere. These are the subsidiary gifts that we get. Religious deeds fill us well in all the four spheres of *Dharma*, *Artha*, *Kāma* and *Moksha*.

तद्यथाम्रफलार्थे निमित्ते छायागन्ध इत्यनूत्पद्येते,
एवं धर्मं चर्यमाणमर्था अनूत्पद्यन्ते।

Tadyathāmraphalārthe nimite chhāyāgandha ityanootapdyete
Yewam dharmam charyamānamarthā anutpadyante

(ii) *Āpastamba Smriti* : *Āpastamba Smriti* contains 10 chapters and 200 *slokas*. It deals mostly with different rituals of expiation, particularly regarding cows. The first chapter deals with the cows — how to look after them, how to serve and which particular act will be treated as a sin.

But it is just the beginning. He has dealt with almost all the common topics of the *Smritis*.

Āpastamba has thought over and taught self-revelation and salvation through it. One, who has control over his heart, mind and senses, and follows a religious path, death cannot disturb him. No one can bring harm to a really religious person:

न यमं यममित्याहुरात्मा वै यम उच्यते।
आत्मा संयमितो येन तं यमः किं करिष्यति।

Na yamam yamamityāhurātmā wai yam uchyate
Ātmā sanyamito yen tam yamah kim karishyati

— *Āpastamba Smriti* (10:3)

He, who follows the scriptures and *Yogashāstras*, has thrown violence out of his life, lives peacefully and works for the betterment of each creature, gets salvation:

मोक्षोभवेत प्रीतिनिवर्तकस्य
अध्यात्मयोगैकरतस्य सम्यक्।
मोक्षो भवेन्नित्यमहिंसकस्य
स्वाध्याययोगागतमानसस्य।

Moksho bhawet preetinibaratakasya
Adhyātmayogaikartasya samyak
Moksho bhawenityamahinsakasya
Swādhyāyayogāgatmānasasya

— *Āpastamba Smriti* (10:7)

Āpastamba is almost angry with anger. 'Almost' because he had no anger left in him. He was all an emblem of patience, tolerance, compassion, forgiveness and all other human and divine qualities. Anger has devastating effect. It destroys one completely. On the other hand, forgiveness is a boon and a creative force. They are the real human beings who are kind, compassionate and tolerant. Only they can sustain during the calamities. The works done under the spell of 'anger' can not bear fruit. For him 'forgiveness' is the greatest quality of a human being:

न तथासिस्तथा तीक्ष्णः सर्पो वा दुरधिष्ठितः।
यथा क्रोधो हि जन्तूनां शरीरस्थो विनाशकः।।
क्षमागुणो हि जन्तूनामिहामुत्र सुखप्रदः।
अरिर्वा नित्यसंक्रुद्धो यथात्मा दुरधिष्ठितः।।

Na tathāsistathā teekshanah sarpo wā duradhishthitah
Yathā krodho hi jantunām sharirastho vināshakah
Chhamāguno hi jantunāmihāmutra sukhpradah
Arirwā nityasankrudho yathātmā duradhishthitah

— *Āpastamba Smriti* (10:4-5)

Along with all these, Āpastamba had drawn the pen-sketch of an enlightened person. It was the most popular among all his oft-quoted lines. He said, "Only he is the visionary, who has self-revelation, who treats the wife of all other persons as his mother, the wealth of all other men as dust, and accepts all other creatures as a replica of his own self":

मातृवत परदारेषु परद्रव्येषु लोष्टवत्।
आत्मवत् सर्वभूतेषु यः पश्यति स पश्यति।।

Mātriwat pardāreshu pardravyeshu loshtawat
Ātmawat sarbabhuteshu yah pashyati sa pashyati

— *Āpastamba Smriti* (10:11)

10. Shankha Smriti

Maharshi Shankha had a younger brother known as Likhit. In the *Shānti Parva* of the great epic *Mahābhārata* there is a revealing story of these two brothers. They had their *āshrams* at the bank of river 'Bāhudā'. Once, Likhit went to the *āshram* of his elder brother Shankha. He saw some ripe mangoes. He plucked a few of them and started eating. In the meantime, Shankha returned. In his opinion, Likhit was a thief. So he asked him to go to King Sudyumna and ask him for punishment. The king forgave him but Likhit insisted on getting punished. He believed that without punishment he would not be purified. At last, the king ordered that both his hands should be cut off. It was done but neither Likhit felt any pain nor was he aggrieved. He returned back to his brother. Maharshi Shankha asked him to go to the river and perform the *tarpan* (offering water) to the ancestors. It was not possible without the hands. Likhit obeyed. He took a bath and the moment he thought of *tarpan* both his hands came out as if they were the original. He completed the ritual, came to his brother and happily showed him his hands. Shankha said, "It was possible because of your expiation and our penance and pious deeds."

Likhit asked, "If it was so, then why did you send me for punishment? If it was so then why did you not punish me yourself? Why did you not purify me earlier?"

Maharshi Shankha answered, "You had broken the code of conduct. Punishment was essential. I would have punished you myself, but it is the duty of the king. My punishing you would have been interference in his work. I would have purified you but only after breaking the general code of conduct. One should never transgress one's limitations."

It is one thing to teach and it is quite a different thing to follow those teachings. We have the teachers but they themselves do not follow those teachings. They have many followers but even the followers do not follow those teachings. Naturally, there is perhaps not a single person in this *Kaliyug* who is free from anxieties, who is happy and healthy and who is peacefully leading a contented life.

Both the brothers have given us many treatises, individual as well as combined. They are the given here:

(i) *Laghushankha Smriti*: It has only 71 *slokas*. The most important among them is the last one in which he clearly says that whenever the conscience of a man starts pinching, the act is irreligious and one should keep on trying for purification with *Gãyatri mantra* and other methods till his conscience does not ask him to stop:

यत्र यत्र संकीर्णं पश्यत्यात्मन्यसंशयम्।
तत्र तत्र तिलैर्होमो गायत्र्यावर्तनं तथा।।

Yatra yatra sankeernam pasyatyātamanyasanshayam
Tatra tatra tilairhomo Gāyatrayāwartanam tathā

— *Laghushankha Smriti* (71)

(ii) *Likhit Smriti*: It is the *Smriti* composed and compiled by Maharshi Likhit. It contains 96 slokas. It says that till the bones of a person remains inside the sacred river Gangā, he himself remains in the Heaven.

(iii) *Shankha Smriti*: Four things are truly essential for people of all the four social divisions. They are forgiveness, truth, pride and purity:

क्षमासत्यं दमः शौचं सर्वेषाम विशेषतः।

Kshamā satyam damah shaucham sarbeshām visheshtah

— *Shankha Smriti* (1:5)

He praises and accepts only such a woman for a wife who is expert in household works, faithful to her husband, lives by him and bears him children:

सा भार्या या गृहे दक्षा सा भार्या या पतिव्रता।
सा भार्या या पतिप्राणा सा भार्या या प्रजावती।।

Sā bhāryā yā grihe dakshā sā bhāryā yā pativratā
Sā bhāryā yā patiprānā sā bhāryā yā prajāwati

— *Shankha Smriti* (4:15)

Maharshi Shankha laid ample stress on yoga. According to him, yoga has the power to give an aim to life, to free us from diseases, anger and lust and from bad company. Yoga absorbs all the bad effects of materialism and worldly life, and draws us towards spiritualism:

प्राणायामैर्दहेदोषान धारणाभिश्च किल्विषम्।
प्रत्याहारैरसत्संगान् ध्यानेनानैश्वरान् गुणान्।।

Prănāyāmairdehedoshān dhāranābhischa kilbisham
Pratyāhārairsatsangān dhyānenānaiswarān gunān

— *Shankha Smriti* (7:12)

(iv) *Shankha-Likhit Smriti*: *Shankha-Likhit Smriti* is a combined and unique effort of both the brothers. It will be a wonder for the Europeans who claim that co-authorship is a novel idea given by the West. They would be surprised to know that such books were written in India thousands of years before Christ was born.

In only 32 *slokas,* they have laid ample stress on the rituals before taking the food and feeding the guests first, on not to eat the food made of cereals given by others and on the duties of a king.

One should not think whether the guest is rich or poor, skilled or unskilled, one should give his guest the best hospitality:

दातार: किं विचारेण गुणवान् निर्गुणी भवेत्।
समं वर्षति पर्जन्य: सस्यादपि तृणादपि।।

Dātārah kim vichāren gunawān nirguni bhawet
Samam varshati parjanyah sasyādapi trinādapi

— *Shankha-Likhit Smriti* (7)

In their eyes, a king has to give security to his subjects. He should ensure the safety of cows, land, the old and weak persons, the orphans, children, saints, Brahmins and those who are being exploited:

गावो भूमिः कलत्रं च ब्रह्मस्वहरणं तथा।
यस्तु न त्रायते राजा तमाहुर्ब्रह्मघातकम्।।

Gāwo bhumih kalatram cha brahmaswaharanam tathā
Yastu na trāyate rājā tamāhurbrahmaghātakam

— *Shankha-Likhit Smriti* (24)

They suggested that the wise men should neither take the cereals from others nor board others' vehicles or airplanes neither wish for others' women nor live in others' house. Such acts take away the wealth, strength, energy, stamina, fertility, confidence and fame etc:

अन्नात् तेजो मनः प्राणांश्चक्षुः श्रोत्रं यशो बलम्।
धृतिं श्रुतिं तथा शुक्रं परान्नं वर्जयेद् बुधः।।
परन्नं परवस्त्रं च परयानं परस्त्रियः।
परवेश्मनि वासश्च शुक्रस्यापि श्रियं हरेत्।।

Annāt tejo manah prānānschakshuh shrotram yasho balam
Dhritim shrutim tathā shukram parānnam varjayed budhah
Parānnam parvastram cha paryānam parstriyah
Parwesmani wāsashcha shukrasyapi shriyam haret

— *Shankha-Likhit Smriti* (16-17)

Purānas

The effect of the Vedas is seen in the books, the *Purānas*. It is said that in the *Purānas*, the Vedas have found full expression and complete analysis — ***Itihāspurānāvyām vedam samupabrihanyet.*** Hence, it is essential to know these great books on life in general and human life in particular, to know the full application of the Vedas because all of them are for life, the most natural life and they ensure the continuity of life on the mother Earth. By looking away from them human beings will be thrown far too away from Nature, which will automatically result in the extinction of life as the very undercurrent eternal system of change and interdependence will be broken.

The *Purānas* have been divided in four groups known as

1. *Mahāpurāna*
2. *Purāna*
3. *Atipurāna*
4. *Upapurāna*

There were originally only 18 *Purānas* which were compiled by Ved Vyās. But it is claimed that in each category, there are 18 *Purānas*. At one stage it is mentioned in ancient books that they were 108 in number. At present, there are more than 300 *Purānas* available. The reason is that when the not so learned pandits were installed as the heads of various temples, they were asked to make changes in the ancient books of knowledge, the scriptures. They may have made changes in other books too, but they found *Purānas* a very convenient place to make the forced changes. They changed them and even composed 'new' *Purānas.* Naturally, their number increased. As they were not so learned and sublime, hence, their language too was not so impressive; it is often reduced to mediocre prose, which is perhaps the only proof that these *Purānas* were written in immediate past and not in the remote past. The general people accept only the original 18 *Mahā Purānas* as the real ones. They are:

(1) *Brāhman Purāna*

(2) *Padam Purāna*

(3) *Vishnu Purāna*

(4) *Shiv Purāna*

(5) *Srimad Bhāgwat Purāna*

(6) *Nārdeeya Purāna*

(7) *Mārkandeya Purāna*

(8) *Agni Purāna*

(9) *Bhabishya Purāna*

(10) *Brahmavaivarta Purāna*

(11) *Linga Purāna*

(12) *Varāh Purāna*

(13) *Kand Purāna*

(14) *Vāman Purāna*

(15) *Kurma Purāna*

(16) *Matsya Purāna*

(17) *Garuda Purāna*

(18) *Brahmānd Purāna*

All the *Purānas* have been written in the form of stories. The stories in themselves seem unbelievable. But *Purānas* are not the modern books of stories. They cannot be taken as fairy tales. They must be read and analysed with utmost devotion and concentration.

Let us take this example:

Sangyā, the daughter of Viswakarmā was married to Surya but was unable to bear the heat. She left him leaving behind a shadow Sangyā and started living in the form of a mare. When the Sun learnt it, he too changed into a horse and started living with her. When Viswakarmā learnt everything, he divided one Sun into Sixteen Suns to considerably reduce the heat.

Now the question arises — how could Sangyā create a duplicate? How can we claim that Sangyā was a human being? Can a human being survive if and when cut into sixteen pieces?

Sangyã has many meanings, but two meanings are popular. Sangyã means sense or consciousness and it also means noun. The story must have deeper meanings than we are able to realise.

Purãnas are the history of Creation, Cosmos, Life, Elements and Energy, all galaxies and all worlds. Hence, they are eternal history. They have been written by sublime and divine figures. They are there since time immemorial. Naturally, they are timeless. Such things equivalent to *Purãnas* have not ever been written by man anywhere else on the earth. They are our heritage and will remain so without any proclamation by anyone.

In other parts of the world, men have tried to replace the old wisdom but success has evaded them. The study of *Purãnas* is often compared to soothing northern rays of the sun, the contents are beehive, the legends are the bees and the wisdom that we get from them is the nectar which gives long life and incomparable happiness. These classic books either have everything that was named as it appears in them or they must be symbolic.

For example:

Bhãrata was in Jambudweepa. But, where is Jambudweepa? There is no such island. It means they must have talking about either the continental plate or the whole of Asian continent which may have been like an island in the remote past.

Skanda Purãna: Sutasamhitã

Skanda Purãna holds a special position among the 18 *Purãnas*, and so it is the most famous and the largest one.

This enormous *Purana* is divided in two groups: *Samhitãs* and Divisions. It contains 6 *Samhitãs* and 50 Divisions. Its second *Samhitã* is called *Sutasamhitã* which has been dictated by Sanata Kumãra: ***ãdyã sanatakumãroktã dwitiyã sutasamhitã.***

Dharma has been taken in its eternal, universal and humanitarian form in the *Sutasamhitã*. In its twentieth chapter known as *Yagyabaibhava,* religion has been discussed in detail and in spiritual terms.

In this context, *Sutasamhitã* divides religion in two types:

- *Samula* (with root)
- *Nirmula* (without root)

स्वमनीषिकायोत्पन्नो निर्मूलो धर्मसंहिता:।
श्रद्धया सहितो यस्तु सोऽपि उदाहृता।।
निर्मूलोऽपि स्वबुद्धैव कल्पितोऽपि महर्षय:।
देवताराधनाकारो धर्म: पूर्वोदिताद्धार:।।

Swamanishikayotpanno nirmulo dharmasangyitah
Shraddhyã sahito yastu soapi dharma udãhrita
Nirmuloapi swabuddhaiwa kalpitoapi maharshayah
Devatãrãdhanãkãro dharmah purvoditãdwarah

(*Religion which is performed according to self-knowledge and feelings with devotion and dedication, is said to be rootless.*

The religion that is followed according to scriptures and is dedicated to gods is religion with root. In this way, the second one is better.)

• Itihās (Epics)

The twin peerless epics, the *Rāmāyana* by Vālmiki and the *Māhabhārata* by Ved Vyās, are the most revered books in the world. The two greatest epics ever composed by human mind have been accepted as the books of history as they deal with the life and thought of an epoch. ***Ādhyātma Rāmāyana*** and ***Yoga Vashishtha*** are also treated as the books of history. They have their own form and versions in every living language of the world. They have slowly travelled to distant lands to influence the local culture. No other book has preached humanism more than these two books. The climax is that even their bad characters, the villains have become heroes in many parts simply because the villains too are wise and very powerful characters.

Most of the people including writers feel the impact of their different characters even without reading the original epics and some of them write books, compose poems and stage plays on the basis of only hearsay material. The greatness of these epics are well established in the heart and mind of the people.

The epics have been discussed in detail in the chapter. *Grantha-trai* in this book.

Darshan

During the ancient times, every disciple had to read the literature first and only after getting mastery over the language and literature, he was asked to read different branches of *Shāstras* (Science) and *Darshan* (Philosophy). Naturally they had a great command over their language. As a result, the books of even botany, mathematics and medicines have all been written in verses or *slokas*. The *sutras* are the most compact and condensed expressions. They express everything precisely. Not even half of the syllable has been wasted.

Philosophy according to the learned Indian saints and sages is:

दृश्यते यथार्थतया वस्तु पदार्थज्ञानमिति दर्शनम्।
सर्वेषां तु स नामानि कर्माणि च पृथक् पृथक्।
वेदशब्देभ्यः एवादौ पृथक् संस्थाश्च निर्ममे।।

Drishyate yathārthatayā vastu padārthajnanamiti darshanam
Sarveshām the sa nāmāni karmāni cha prithak prithak
Vedashabdebhya aiwādau prithak samsthāscha nirmame

— *Manusmriti* (1:21)

(That which gives knowledge of the inner essence of the matter and show the reality is called Darshan or philosophy.)

A philosopher is the one who has attained wisdom and knows the elements. Philosophy deals with the Creation, cause, effect and continuity of life and shows the meaning and purpose behind every object and being. Indian philosophy has been divided into six main divisions and each of them have been divided in many sub-divisions because of the *āchāryas* who taught them. A slight deviation from the original in its perception and delineation gave birth to a different branch of philosophy. The original six are:

1. *Vaisheshika Darshan*
2. *Sānkhya Darshan*
3. *Yoga Darshan*
4. *Nyāya Darshan*
5. *Poorva Mimāmsā Darshan*
6. *Uttar Mimāmsā Darshan*

There are hundreds of original books on them and a few books on each of them to explain and elucidate them. They are known as *Teekā* or *Bhāshya* (commentary).

Nyāya and ***Vaisheshika Darshan*** lay emphasis on an acute logical analysis of language and the different processes of thought, developing a terminology for precision of statement. This has become the language of philosophical discussions.

The original systems express 'motive and ideas' which are truly practical. They all aim at a state of perfection beyond suffering. In a nutshell, the basic common attitude of all these Indian systems is to be free from suffering and get salvation. All of them show, in different ways, how philosophy can help men know the cause of suffering, and how knowledge can help them forsake suffering and attain perfect peace. All of them believe and claim that true and effective knowledge cannot be attained by mere study. Moral and physical discipline, control and piety must accompany study, reasoning, intense concentration and repeated meditation on the philosophical truths. The action must show the purity of nature and character.

Law of Karma

The Indian systems are more than theoretical discussions. They are the ways of moulding life in accordance with different views and perspectives. That immortality and perfection in releasing from bondage and giving salvation is so luring that millions of people still follow the Vedic and Vedantic philosophy. This is because in spite of their theoretical differences, all of them insist upon a common pattern of intellectual, physical and moral discipline, which make them all 'Indian'. *It is the unity of moral outlook.*

The most common theoretical component of this outlook is the conviction sustained by different arguments, that the constitution of the world is MORAL, that the actions of men determine the course of events in Nature as well as in the mind. The moral worth of every action is preserved so that everyone gets his due here or hereafter. This belief is popularly known as the Law of *karma* and is accepted by both the theists and the atheists. But only the law of the past *karma* does not determine everything. The present life in its beginning is determined by the past but it can be changed for worse or better by present effort. The future will be an award (*puraskāra*) for the action (*purushārtha*). This gives immense power to man who is the architect of his own destiny, who can make or mar it with his morally pure or impure action.

Sānkhya Darshan propounds a dualistic metaphysic of souls and Nature, and the possibility of the liberation of the soul from its bondage to Nature. For freedom, it can practise detachment. The *Purusha* and *Prakriti* are the two constituent principles of creation. The *ajā* (unborn) *Pradhāna* (a subtle and casual condition) has three *gunas* (qualities) known as *satva* (pure), *rājas* (royal) and *tamas* (demonic).

Yoga Darshan goes deep into the psychology of attention and concentration, and lays down a practical path to liberation by gradual concentration of attention on the nature of the soul, aided by physical culture, moral discipline and meditative and physical exercises. Yoga accepts meditation and reasoning, based on eight limbs — *yama*, *niyama*, *āsana*, *pranāyāma*, *pratyāhāra*, *dhāranā*, *dhyāna* and *samādhi*, as the means for union which is the goal of every being.

There are many benefits of yoga if it is treated as a philosophy and not just health exercise. Yoga gives strength and flexibility, releases stress, keeps mentally and physically healthy, purifies body and mind, and keeps one on the right track. It increases the ability to reflect on the past and perceive the future, gives courage and resolution to perform rare tasks, prepares one to help others. *Yoga is looking within*. With introspection, awareness grows that leads to harmony with others. That way, systematically and surely Yoga leads to final Union with the Absolute God.

1. ॐ

Yoga is an Indian *Darshan*, a way of seeing,
A precise and classical path of inside moving.
Yoga is a tangible Metaphysical Methodology;
Yoga is ultimately the Soul's and God's meeting.

2. ॐ

Yoga makes one see oneself with greater clarity,
Full of life and spirit, Yoga gives enough vivacity,
By yoking and joining Individual Soul to Universal Spirit;
Yoga keeps shapely, checks thinness and obesity.

3. ॐ

Health and fitness is needed for transcending,
For remaining empty-minded and for meditating,
Still outwardly but moving inside very fast;
It climbs the airy ladder, steadily ascending.

4. ॐ

It purifies blood for stronger and durable cells,
To be able to bear life's vales, dales and gales.
It helps in absorbing and storing cosmic energy;
With rhythmic force in inner space, it always sails.

5. ॐ

Yoga is mental and physical in equal proportion,
It remakes and gives shape to each distortion.
It urges, makes earnest appeal for complete piety;
For which lays powerful condition and extortion.

(From Yoga in Spiritual Quadruplets)

The ***Mimāmsā*** is a philosophic justification of Vedic rituals. ***Purva Mimāmsā*** deals with the *karma* (ritualistic) part of the Vedas which are taken as a means of validating knowledge. Knowledge leads to final emancipation which depends on *naimitya karma*. It believes that *Brahman* can be known through scriptures and meditation.

Uttara Mimāmsā is the *jnāna* (knowledge) part of the Vedas. It too accepts Vedas as valid means of knowledge. The world is an apparent *vivarta* (transformation) through *māyā*. It is not the reality. Knowledge is the only way of *mukti* or liberation from the endless cycle of birth and death.

Mimāmsā and *Vedānta* are both based on the teachings of Vedas and Upanishads. **Vedānta** is the search of *Brahman* through the self and emancipation of the soul through knowledge, meditation and virtuous deeds.

• Bhãshya: Teekã: Sectarian

Somehow, it seems, that the learned men stopped thinking something new and useful. Unfortunately they all confined themselves to the explanations of the established *sutras*, *mantras*, and treatises. In order to conclude one debate, they started another debate, and in place of freely and openly mixing to one or the other lineage, they started creating new 'sects'. Already divided Hindus were further divided into different sects and sub-sects. Although this phase was the most important phase in Hinduism as those wise men were able to save and keep the morale, religion, culture and the books of wisdom and scriptures, as they worked with one objective in mind—to 'save'. They did not think of the after effects. They had neither time nor space. They were not as free and secure as the *rishis* and *munis* of the yesteryears. If there was any demonic attack on the *rishis* and *munis*, the rulers were there to protect them. But during the middle ages, the position was reversed. The rulers were the demons who with determined intention were trying their toughest best to destroy them. There was no way the Indians could exchange views or make united efforts to deal with their atrocities. They found the separatist way to remain united in parts. They might have thought to join back as and when the better days arrive. As a result, thousands of religious leaders came up and established a sect each in their respective area. They accepted everyone in their folds to stop forced conversion.

They loudly proclaimed that the Supreme God in all the forms is in Hinduism, so people need not accept some other religion. They can worship *Nirgun* or *Sagun*, *Brahman* or Krishna, Shiva or Ram, Hari or Vishnu, Buddha or Mahavir. They can be *Vaishnav* or *Shakt*. They can remain among the *Nath* or the *Bhaktas*, or can simply show their devotion and pray.

It is extremely difficult for the younger generation and the people of the world born decades after independence to understand the dangers on the life and existence of the Indians which started in around 7th century AD, enslaved us in the 10th century AD and the slavery continued for one thousand long years. That was the time when they were forced to keep the girls and womenfolk safe under curtains, marry their daughters off as early as possible, even during childhood and burnt the widows inhumanely on pyres of their husbands, even collectively to save their honour. Such things were totally alien to us. We originally belong to a very free society of *gandharvas, apsarās,* and *swayamvars*. So, the moment we got a chance, we totally freed the society from *bāl-vivāh, pardā-prathā* and *sati-prathā*.

In the face of such destructions and devastations, people remained united in parts or kept a part united under one banner or under one religious leader. Naturally that was the time of prolific writing, composition of religious songs, of *sādhus* and *mahātmās* and of *satsang* and debates. Treatises were written as a response to every book that was known as a part of the Vedas. They had their preferences quite clear that the Vedas and all their books of knowledge and scriptures have to be saved. They were praised and respected for all their efforts. They were great and they deserve all the reverence that we or the coming generation can show to them. We bow our head and prostrate before them.

The books that came during that long period are thousands in number because each sect produced their own books. The books on Buddhism and Jainism alone both religious and literary are thousands in number. Each sect that claimed to be a way of life had different books. They are wrongly claimed to be separate people. As the Hinduism is individualistic in its approach, so all of them are branches, and since the growth of population has touched an unbelievably new height, so each sect has a substantial number of followers. Naturally, their existence can neither be denied nor wiped out. As Indians have come up with numerous ways of spirituality, worship, devotion and pious deeds, so they have existed and can exist simultaneously together. There will be virtually no problem whatsoever, if they treat themselves an integral part of the Whole and keep themselves engrossed in humanitarian deeds. The only essential thing is that everyone should think and try to ensure the continuity of life on the earth and to make it a better place to live in. That is the whole purpose behind religion and scriptures. Those who deviate from their path have no religion and need no scripture.

Commentaries

Given here are important books among those sectarian and explanatory *Granthas*, which are popularly known as commentaries:

(i) *Advaitvãd* by Sri Shankarãchãrya

(ii) *Vishishthãdvait* by Sri Ramãnujãchãrya

(iii) *Dvaitãdvait* by Sri Nimbakãchãrya

(iv) *Shuddhãdvait* by Sri Ballabhãchãrya

(v) *Dvaitvad* by Sri Madhvãchãrya

(vi) *Achintyavedãvedavãd* by Sri Godiyãchãrya

Nibandha Granthas

The *Nibandha Granthas* are also treated as the *Smritis* though they are believed to have been written during the middle ages, under the active supervision and pressure of the ruler class. That is the reason that they were not allowed an independent existence and were accepted as only a part of the *Smriti Granthas*. They all aim at giving details of the different religious acts, rites and rituals. The essayists have tried hard to explain the apparently not clear meanings of the ancient treatises. In other words, they have tried to raise different doubts to mislead the masses. Most of them are voluminous too. They could not gain popularity, but are still among the least known books. Later on, they were given additional support by others with books of 'Meanings and Explanations'; but one book by Kamalākar Bhatta of Kāshi *Vivādtāndav* (*The Deadly Dance of Debate*) is enough to make everything clear.

These middle ages *Nibandha Granthas* are only explanatory notes on the different *Smritis*. As these men were not as wise, pious, illuminated and sublime visionary sages as the *rishis*, so their personal whims, mundane concepts, social and cultural prejudices found expression in the essays. They should be read with an open mind and caution. One must detect digressions and misleading or erroneous conclusions and leave them as and where they are. They should not be discussed, explained or studied forward. One must depend on the original ancient *Granthas* for true knowledge.

Some of the important *Nibandha Granthas* are mentioned below:

(1) *Dāyabhāg* by Jeemootbāhan

(2) *Kālvivek* by Jeemootbāhan

(3) *Vāyawahārmātrika* by Jeemootbāhan
(4) *Smritivivek* by Shoolpāni (4 volumes)
(5) *Smrititatva* by Raghunandan (28 volumes)
(6) *Hārlatā* by Aniruddha
(7) *Āshouchvivaran* by Aniruddha
(8) *Pitridayitā* by Aniruddha
(9) *Āchārsāgar* by Ballāl Sen
(10) *Pratisthāsāgar* by Ballāl Sen
(11) *Udbhutsāgar* by Ballāl Sen
(12) *Ācharadarshan* by Sridutta Upādhyāya
(13) *Samaypradeep* by Sridutta Upādhyāya
(14) *Shrādhkalā* by Sridutta Upādhyāya
(15) *Smriti Ratnākar* by Chandeswar
(16) *Vivādchintāmani* by Vāchaspati Mishra
(17) *Smritichandrikā* by Devanbhatta
(18) *Chaturvarga Chintāmani* by Hemādri (Encyclopaedia)
(19-24) 7 books by Mādhvāchārya
- *i.* *Kālmādhav*
- *ii.* *Parāshermādhav*
- *iii.* *Dattakmimāmsa*
- *iv.* *Gotrapravar Nirnaya*
- *v.* *Muhurtamādhav*
- *vi.* *Smritisangrah*
- *vii.* *Vrātyastomapadhati*

(25-28) 4 books by Nandapandit

i. *Shrādhkalplatā*

ii. *Shuddhichandrika*

iii. *Tatwamuktāwali*

iv. *Dattakmimāmsa*

(29-31) 3 books by Narāyan Bhatta

i. *Tristhalisetu*

ii. *Antyesthipadhati*

iii. *Prayogratnākar*

(32-38) Out of the 22 books by Kamlākar Bhatta, only these seven are important:

i. *Nirnayasindhu*

ii. *Shoodrakamalākar*

iii. *Dānkamalākar*

iv. *Poortakamalākar*

v. *Vedaratna*

vi. *Prayāschitaratna*

vii. *Vivādtāndava*

(39) *Bhagwantabhāskar* by Neelkantha Bhatta

(40) *Veermitrayodaya* by Veer Mitra

(41) *Kalpataru* by Laxmidhar

(42) *Vivādārnava* by Jagannātha Tarkapanchānan (Law-book)

(43) *Dharmasindhu* by Kāshināth Upādhyāya

(44) *Nirnyāmrita* by Kāshināth Uādhyāya

(45) *Purushārtha Chintāmani* by Kāshināth Upādhyāya

Āgam Granthas

Most of the sects followed the main book written by their leaders. Each genuine leader in each century wrote books with great devotion and fair intention. Even the *tāntriks* came up with their own books, which known as *Āgam* or *Tantra Granthas*. They have been derived from the Vedas, hence they are called *Āgam* while all the earlier divisions from Vedas to Commentaries are called *Nigam*. In *Sanātan Dharma* or the Eternal Religion both the *Āgams* and the *Nigams* are accepted as authentic.

The *Āgam Granthas* are divided into two distinct divisions '*Dakshināgam*' or '*Samaymatta*' (Rightist) and '*Vāmāgam*' or '*Kaulmatta*' (Leftist). They are further divided into *Vaishanvāgam*, *Shaivāgam* and *Shāktāgam*.

1) Vaishnavāgam

Vaishnavāgam is revered as sacred and authentic as the *Smritis*. They deal with the appearance, qualities and works of the gods and try to revive different *mantrās* devoted or related to those gods. In *Vaishnavāgam* alone, there are two types of *Granthas*. One is known as *Pānchrātra Samhitā* and the other one is called *Vaikhānas Āgam*. The *Pānchrātra Samhitās* are more important than the other one. Only the following 13 *Samhitās* are available in *Pānchrātra Samhitā*:

(i) *Ahirbudhanya Samhitā*

(ii) *Jayākhya Samhitā*

(iii) *Parāsher Samhitā*

(iv) *Kapilanjal Samhitā*

(v) *Ishwar Samhitā*

(vi) *Pādmyatantra Samhitā*

(vii) *Brihadbrahma Samhitā*

(viii) *Bhāradwaj Samhitā*

(ix) *Vishnu Samhitā*

(x) *Shriprashna Samhitā*

(xi) *Vishnutilaka Samhitā*

(xii) *Sātwat Samhitā*

(xiii) *Lakshmi Samhitā*

2) Shaivāgam

In *Shaivāgam,* it is held that originally all the 28 main *tantrās* appeared through the mouth of Lord Shiva which have grown up to 64 while they become 208 when the *up-tantrās* were added to them. But most of them have perished and only a few are available. Out of them, the following 13 are very important:

(i) *Pāshupatsutra*

(ii) *Nareshwarparikshā*

(iii) *Ratnātraya*

(iv) *Nādkārikā*

(v) *Tatvaprakāshikā*

(vi) *Tatvasangrah*

(vii) *Shrutisuktimālā*

(viii) *Bhogakārikā*

(ix) *Mokshakārikā*

(x) *Tātparyasangrah*

(xi) *Tatvatraya*

(xii) *Parmokshanirāshkārikā*

(xiii) *Suttasamhitā*

There are many books based on the *Shiva Sutra*, particularly in the *Pratyavimārga* which has 92 authentic *Āgam Granthas* but they give utmost importance to the following *'Trik'* (three):

(i) *Nāmaktantra*

(ii) *Mālinitantra*

(iii) *Sidhāntatantra*

On the other hand, the *Veershaiva* branch of *Shaivāgam* has equal number of books but treats the following book as the most important:

(i) *Siddhāntashikhāmani*

The following are the other important books of *Shaivāgam* Sect:

(i) *Shivadrishti*

(ii) *Spandsarvaswa*

(iii) *Tribriti*

(iv) *Parātrinshikā*

(v) *Shiddhatrayee*

(vi) *Ishwarpratyabhigyakārikā*

(vii) *Shivastrotrāwali*

(viii) *Tantraloka*

3) Shāktāgam

The *Trigunas* (three perennial qualities), *Satva*, *Raj* and *Tama*, do exist in all human beings. Often they are treated as separate beings, like *Sātvik* as godly or divine, *Rājsik* as ruler or luxury-loving and *Tāmsik* as the demons with deadly instinct. It is also claimed that each human being is born with all the three instincts, nature, qualities, inner-self and psychology, and that every human being is wild, cruel and uncultured like the demons, materialist, luxury-loving, sensual like the rulers, and also divine, full of love, compassion, kindness and other sublime qualities like saints. It is up to an individual to subdue the demonic instincts and spirit and develop his inner-self to incorporate all the divine qualities. If an individual does so then that person is released from the incessant cycle of life, death and rebirth. There are thousands of books which deal with demonic instinct. These *Granthas* are known as *Shāktāgam*. Out of the thousands of books in that tradition, only 64 *Granthas* are treated as the main treatises.

But even they are not available. Only a few *Upanishads* and *Shāstras* are found. The following are the most important among the **Vāmāgam:**

(i) *Kaulopanishad*
(ii) *Arunopanishad*
(iii) *Advaitbhāvopanishad*
(iv) *Tāropanishad*
(v) *Tripuropanishad*
(vi) *Brahichopanishad*
(vii) *Bhāvanopanishad*
(viii) *Kālikopanishad*

The following 8 books are the basic books of *Mishramārga.*

(i) *Durwāsā*
(ii) *Chandrak*
(iii) *Barhaspatya*
(iv) *Jyotsrāwati*

(v) *Bhubneswari*

(vi) *Kalānidhi*

(vii) *Kuleshwari*

(viii) *Kulārnava*

The following 5 *Samhitās* are accepted as authentic treatises of ***Samayāchār***. They are different from the *Nigam Samhitās* of the same name. These are known as '*Shubhāgampanchak*'.

(i) *Vashishtha Samhitā*

(ii) *Sanak Samhitā*

(iii) *Shuka Samhitā*

(iv) *Sananda Samhitā*

(v) *Sanatkumār Samhitā*

The following are the main books for *tāntrik sādhanā* by the followers of *Shāktāgam*:

(i) *Kulārnava*

(ii) *Kulachurāmani*

(iii) *Tantrarāja*

(iv) *Shaktisangamtantra*

(v) *Kālivilās*

(vi) *Gyānārnava*

(vii) *Nāmkeswar*

(viii) *Mahānirvāna*

(ix) *Rudrayamal*

(x) *Tripurārahasya*

(xi) *Dakshināmurti Samhitā*

(xii) *Prapanchsār*

(xiii) *Shardātilak*

(xiv) *Mantramahārnava* (An encyclopaedia of *Tantra*)

6

Nitishāstras

When the great Bhishma Pitāmah was lying on the painful bed of arrows waiting for an auspicious moment to die so that Hastināpur could remain safe and secure, he was asked by the Pāndavas about the birth of the kings. To this, Bhishma said:

"Earlier there was neither a king nor a kingdom, not even the word king. Everything was based on piety and pious deeds. Everyone helped each other. Everything worked on spontaneous *dharma*. There was no fear and no wrong act. All obeyed Nature and worked with natural instinct. But soon lust took over. Desires grew. People started disobeying elders. They did not like the study of Vedas. They stopped performing *yajnas*.

"Gods were worried to see it. It was obviously degeneration of values. They went to Brahmā and explained the problem. Brahmā consoled them and promised them to do something. After consoling them, he closed his eyes and meditated over the matter. He opened his eyes and informed them that he has created a new scripture from his own mind to guide the people. It had one lakh chapters. These chapters could have been *slokas* because there are many great *granthas* with one lakh *slokas*:

ततो अध्याय सहस्त्राणां शतं चक्रे स्वबुद्धिजम

Tato adhyāya sahastrānāma shatam chakre swabudhjam

— *Mahābhārata, Shānti Parva* (59:29)

Bhishma stopped for some time to take rest, then he spoke again:

"The new scripture is called ***Nitishāstra***. It includes the directives regarding the *Vedatrai*, and has the *jnāna-kānda*, the *karma-kānda*, agriculture and commerce, and the rules and laws for punishment:

त्रै चान्विक्षिकी चैव वार्ता च भरतर्षभ:।
दण्डनीतिश्च विपुला विद्यास्तत्र निर्देशित:।।

Trai chānwikshiki chaiwa vārtā cha Bharatarshabha
Dandanitishcha vipulā vidyāstatra nirdeshita

— *Mahābhārata, Shānti Parva* (59:33)

"It includes the four percepts, *Dharma*, *Artha*, *Kāma* and *Moksha*.

धर्माश्चार्थाश्च कामश्च मोक्षश्च अत्र अनुवर्णिता।

Dharmashchārthascha kāmashcha mokshashcha
atrā anuvarnitā

— *Mahābhārata, Shānti Parva* (59:72)

"Along with them, it includes the ways and means that the world is not derailed from its true path. All such things have been well described in this treatise created by Brahmā:

यैर्यैरूपायैर्लोकस्तु न चलेदार्यवर्त्मनः।
तत् सर्वे राजशार्दूल नीतिशास्त्रेऽभिवर्जितम्।।

Yaiyairrupāyairlokastu na chaledāryavartamanah
Tatsarvam rājashārdula nitishāshtre abhivarnitam

— *Mahābhārata, Shānti Parva* (59:74)

"So the sons of Pāndu! That scripture describes the laws of punishment, justice, history, penance, knowledge, non-violence, service to the old, charity, purity, kindness, compassion. *Yajna*, voyages and the rights and duties of kings have also been described. What can I say more? Everything that is on this earth and inside has been described by Brahmā in that scripture:

भुवि चाधोगतं यच्छ सर्वं दमर्पितं।
तस्मिन् पितामहे शस्त्रे पाण्डवातन ना संशयः।।

Bhuvi chādhogatam yachcha sarvam damarpitam
Tasmin paitāmahe shāshtre pāndavatan na sanshayah

This way and in that immense form, the moral and ethical treatise started its journey of myriads of years, and finally, was handed over to man. The greatest wonder is that in place of keeping it safe, reading, explaining and following the dictates, modern man has forgotten it. The men of the ancient times and the middle ages kept the teachings alive and followed them. There is ample proof of their interest in the form of many books that they wrote and taught in the congregations.

Very few know that Shiva stands for morality and *Shivatatwa* means moral element. In the trio of *Satyam*, *Shivam* and *Sundaram*, *Satyam* is the truth, *Shivam* is morality and *Sundaram* is aesthetics.

Brahmã had some reservations: Who can keep that *Nitishãstra*? Who is *Nitigya*? Who can make others follow the ethical path and lead a life full of moral values?

After much deliberation, he handed the *Nitishãstra* to Lord Shiva. Later on, in order to make it easier for others to memorise, Shiva shortened the book. His new *Nitishãstra* was called ***Vishãlãksha*** for only a big and alert eye could keep everything in view. *Vishãlãksha* contained ten thousand chapters (*slokas*).

For safe keeping and use, Shiva gave *Vishãlãksha* to Indra. Indra too condensed it and gave it to others for memorising, so it was called ***Bãhudãntaka***. It contained only five thousand chapters (*slokas*).

Ãchãrya Brihaspati again shortened it and it came to be known as ***Brihaspati Niti***.

None of the above mentioned books are now available but all of them have been quoted in the *Mahãbhãrata* and

Purānas. Some of their teachings have also been incorporated in the *Mahābhārata.*

Most of the *slokas* were re-written by both Shukrāchārya and Vidur. They are known as ***Shukra Niti*** and ***Vidur Niti.*** These two books are available.

The available *Shukrāchārya Niti* is divided into following *Prakarans*:

- *Rājyakritādhikāra*
- *Yuvarāja Lakshana*
- *Nripa-Rāshtra Lakshan*
- *Suhrida Nirupana*
- *Kosha Nirupana*
- *Vidyā and Kalā Nirupana*
- *Lokadharma Nirupana*
- *Rājadsharma Nirupana*
- *Durga Nirupana*
- *Senā Nirupana*

• Khila Niti Nirupana

Some of the findings and teachings of Shukrāchārya are so great that the combined knowledge of the modern psychologists and sociologists cannot compete with them. The most wonderful thing is that these statements came myriads of years ago:

Naikah sukhi na sartra vistrabdho na cha shankitah

(Do not enjoy pleasure alone, do not have faith on all, and do not get suspicious of all.)

His one teaching is such that the modern materialistic world will never obey and hence never get peace and happiness. It is the age of crime and deliberately causing loss and inflicting pain to others. As a result, all are forced to face loss and endure pain and suffering.

Shukrāchārya said:

कुतेन व्यवहार्यम् तु वृतिलोपम ना कस्यचित्।
न कुर्यात् चिन्तयेत् कस्य मानसाप्यहितम क्वचित्।।

Kutena vyawahāram tu vritilopam na kasyachit
Na kuryāt chintayet kasya manasāpyahitam kwachit

— *Shukra Niti* (3:157-8)

(Do not deceive others, do not destroy others' livelihood, inflicting injury is a very serious matter, do not ever think of causing pain to others.)

Vidur Niti also forms a part of the *Mahābhārata.* Mostly it is in the form of dialogues. Many versions are available in the market and the chapters in them are divided into different ways. They are not all similar in the selection of *slokas,* the content and form. These are, in a way, the moral teachings of Ved Vyās, but there is one peculiarity about him. All his teachings are known either by the books he composed or by the names of the characters. His name is usually not mentioned while quoting him.

The *Mahābhārata* (including the *Gita*), *Rāmāyana*, and many other *granthas* are rich in moral teachings, but they are not treated among the books of *Niti,* even though, their sayings are vehemently quoted.

Niti

The word *niti* has many meanings. It means to carry and deliver, to show, to lead and to teach ways: ***neeyate sanlabhyante upādāya iti wā.***

By presenting some universal truth, the moral teachings guide the people.

सर्पः क्रूरः खलः क्रूरः सर्पात् क्रूरताः खलः।
मन्त्रः औषधि वशः सर्पः खलः केना निवारयेत्।।

Sarpah krurah khalah krurah sarpat krurtarah khalah
Mantra aushadhi bashah sarpah khalah kena niwārate

(The serpents and bad elements are cruel, but the bad elements are worse than the serpents because serpents and their poison can be controlled by mantras and medicine, but there is no way out from the bites of the bad elements.)

To lead one's life according to the dictates of the scriptures is called *niti*: ***niti shāstrena vartanam.***

According to Sanskrit Grammar, suffix *ti* is added to *ni* which means to take, to make or to move ahead. In this way, the word *niti* is created. Somehow all the *shāstras* are closely related to *Nitishāstra*.

Nitishāstra means the science that helps to distinguish wholesome and unwholesome deeds.

The action is the most important thing in life: ***āchārah prathamo dharmah***. Action and behaviour are the first religions. Only study is not important: ***Āchārheenah na punanti vedah***. The scriptures must be followed in life. A person who has read the Vedas, but has not followed the teachings in his life is the worst person. He cannot get purged.

Numerous specialised *Niti Granthas* are still available in Sanskrit. Most of these books contain moral and ethical teachings in the most condensed and appropriate form of *sutras*. They aim at making life happy, pleasant, peaceful, refined, cultured and sublime for achieving divinity and final emancipation and salvation.

They are presented in a rich and simple style which makes the understanding and memorising easier, so that everyone can keep the ideas in mind and quote them whenever needed.

They teach us directly in couplets and indirectly through symbolic and moral tales.

As per our Indian culture: ***Atithi devo bhawah*** (the guests are gods). Here is a tale of Maharshi Mudgala which proves the above saying. Maharshi Mudgala stands for those who treat their guests as gods.

In ancient times, the *rishis* lived far away from the society and social disturbances. That does not mean that they had no family. On the contrary, most of the *rishis* had their family which grew larger over the years so much that today every Indian claims that he/she belongs to the family of one or the other *rishi*. Maharshi Mudgala too lived away from the cacophonous sound of the *janapadas* to remain freely engrossed in meditation and devotion to the Absolute God.

Rishi Mudgala had a great way of living. They used to collect the grains fallen in fields after the harvest, which was called *shila* and also the grains fallen outside the closed grain shop which was called *uchchha*.

Rishi Mudgala had two other personal rules – one was that they would not store more than 34 *seers* (one equivalent to two and a half kilogram) at a time and the other one was that they would cook and eat meal only on the new moon or full moon nights. Even in those times, they kept fast food ready mostly in the form of *sattu* (flour of baked grain). It was enough for them to give energy needed for the body to sustain itself. Rest of the time was utilised in singing devotional songs and helping others.

'On one full moon night, Maharshi Durvāsā, known for his anger, came to Mudgala. The family welcomed him and requested him to partake simple food at their household. Durvasa accepted the invitation and he relished the simple food. He ate away all that was ready for the family. The other members did not try to cook more meal and decided to take the next meal on the coming full moon night.

Durvāsā was satisfied and pleased. He blessed them and went away. But since he liked the food, he returned back on the next full moon night. The same story was repeated. Again, there was nothing left for the Mudgala family. This happened on four consecutive full moon nights and the Mudgala family did not eat a grain for three months in a row.

On the last occasion, in the presence of Durvāsā, a *vimāna* came to take the Mudgala family to heaven. Mudgala enquired about heaven, and after knowing every detail, he declined the offer saying that dissatisfaction, lust and luxury were all there. It was not the suitable place for them. It is needless to state that the Mudgala family got salvation, bliss and beatitude.

The *Nitishāstras* say that lust and luxury spoil the life. We need to control them by controlling our senses. The following tale shows how easily one can be swept off by physical and material illusory needs, and how we can grow strong by freeing ourselves from those lusts and mean demands of the physical self.

Virupa Kapil was the son of the *Rājapurohita* (head priest) of Kaushambi. He was living at the *āshram* of Āchārya Indradutta in Shrāwasti to complete his studies. His meals were arranged at the residence of the *Nagarseth* (the richest man of the town). The maid who served him meal there was extremely beautiful. He was first attracted by her immense beauty, then he fell in love with her. On the occasion of the *Vasant Panchami* Spring Festival) she demanded new clothes and gold ornaments. It was not possible so she suggested a way.

She said that the king of Shrāwasti gaves gold in charity every morning to the very first person who met him. Kapil thought of taking that charity. He planned well to be the first man to meet the king. Early in the evening, he entered the palace and hid himself. He waited throughout the night. Before the dawn, he came out of his hideout but was caught. As the royal gate was not yet opened so he was thought to be a thief. He was arrested and presented before the king.

There he claimed the charity. The king wanted to know, how and why he was hiding inside the palace. Kapil narrated the whole story. The king was pleased with him. He said, "You can ask anything. You will get it." Kapil thought that the usual charity of two grams of gold would be too little to ask, two kilograms of gold might help him but would not last long. Since he had the opportunity, he could secure something to lead a comfortable life. At last he decided and said, "Give me your kingdom."

"With all pleasure, take the kingdom. I have no son. I was looking for an heir. You have demanded the kingdom. Maybe you are the right person to rule here, because you are young and truthful. Now I can go for a long awaited penance. Come on, take your seat on the throne, the ceremony will be completed right now. You have freed me from the illusion and lust. You have rendered me a great service."

Kapil was thinking fast. What was he doing? What was he getting? His lust had grown so high that in place of feeling satisfied with two grams of gold, he had demanded the whole kingdom.

Immediately he said, "O king, you have helped me out of misfortune. I had grown weak. I had become a slave to lust and luxury. You have opened my eyes. Keep your kingdom. I don't want it, because I don't need it now."

When he came out of the court, he was happy. He had neither lust nor illusion. He was a free man.

Continuous Growth

Although, the contribution of modern men to scriptures and Sanskrit language and literature, is quite insignificant yet they boast of its wealth always in the superlative degree.

There is a definite reason behind that. Starting from the *rishis* till the middle ages there was no corner of the Universe and life that they had not described in it. The innumerous dedicated thinkers gave their all to it. The richness was the ultimate result of the devotion and concentrated labour. It was a combined effort too. Hence, despite the fact that more than 80% of its writing was destroyed, yet the remaining 20% was enough to weigh more than the combined knowledge of the world which was to a great extent just a pile of information. Particularly, the people of ancient India touched every worth-mentioning topic and brought out its essence. They expressed them exquisitely well in extremely compact and beautiful language which opened options and had layers of meanings.

This is true of one of its rich branches *Nitishāstras* too, which contains everything from serious to satirical, from couplets to complete poems and epics, and teaches people what to do and what not to do, how to live and how to save oneself and the community during upheaval and at the time of natural or man-made calamity. Most of them are certainly direct in their teachings. *Smritis* are such *Granthas* which aim at directly asking the people to do this and not to do that, which is known as *karmākarma viveka*. *Upanishads* are also full of such moral teachings.

To the Indian thinkers, causes and effects were more important than date and place. Dates and places have importance in the immediate past, present and near future but when myriads of years pass, they lose their significance, and only the cause and its effect remain in some apparent or hidden form. The great *rishis* and thinkers have written mostly on the numerous causes and their infinite effects. Both the great epics of pre-historical India, the *Rāmāyana* and the *Mahābhārata*, are living examples. So, the dates and places related to those men of worldly, sublime and divine knowledge have neither been mentioned nor are known. In fact, it makes little difference whether the battle of *Mahābhārata* was fought in Pānipat or Sonepat, in Punjab or Haryana or in the Thar Desert. It has little or no significance. The wars had their personal and general causes. They taught the Indians the meaning of existence. They added value to their existence and meaning to their deeds and tried their best to avoid misdeeds and the resultant misfortune and pain. They readily and happily turned towards moral culture and moral living.

A simple incident, which is very complex and meaningful, is usually narrated to give an insight into the working of life and the existence. A man was being chased by an elephant. He was tired of running and the elephant was coming closer. The fear of being caught and crushed was lurking large over him. He saw a dead and dry well. He jumped into it. While in the air, he got a glimpse of many snakes moving at the bottom. He found a thick branch of a big banyan tree. He caught it. Now he was in a more precarious position. The elephant from above was trying to catch him with its trunk. Below the snakes were hissing. Then he saw that the thick branch that he was holding was not safe either. One black and another white rat were cutting the branch. Just then, he heard some music from above. He looked up. There was a big honeycomb. A drop of honey fell down on a nearby leaf. The man licked it. It gave him immense strength.

Such is life, which is the essence of all *Nitishāstras*, the moral and ethical teaching. The life is based solely on such cause and effect. The meaning of life is revealed here. It is the best symbolic story that teaches the truth, shows our existence and gives us its meaning.

The man, in the story, represents life that is being chased by problems represented by the elephant. He finds a shelter in the form of well. He feels safe and secure in the well. But there is no security as the death in the form of snakes is always lurking there. There is no escape from death. It is not the end. The time is fleeting away. Days (white rat) and nights (black rat) are bringing us closer to our end. Under such circumstances, he gets a drop of honey, the nectar of life. That one drop of nectar gives bliss and eternal happiness to him. What more one needs to know? The whole truth of life is symbolically presented here. If we can understand it, then we can be sure of getting the nectar; if not, then the most simple and general mortal end is known to all.

Taking birth, living life, doing deeds and meeting the ultimate end are integral part of life. The dates and places have no importance in this. In the same way, when this was story created has little significance. It teaches a very significant lesson and that is what is more important.

This is one definite reason that the dates have been deliberately left out. Another reason is that all the dates have become controversial as many scholars have given irrefutable logic and proof about different dates. Moreover, it is not important to give dates to myths or to something that looks great, attractive and mysterious like a myth.

Nĩtĩ Granthas

From the Vedic Period till 1200 AD, *Niti Sloka* and *Niti Sukta* remained as a mode and form of expression and the strongest device to teach. The Vedas, Brahmã, Vishnu, Shiva, Rãma, Krishna, Vyãs, Brihaspati, Shukra, Indra, Mãrkandeya, Bhãradwãj, Vaishampãyan, Buddha, Mahavira, Chãnakya, Bhartrihari, Nanak, Kabir, Tulsi and Rahim and many more, all have added something valuable to the Science of Ethics and enriched it. But all these writers have taken a lot from the Vedas, *Smritis* and from the two renowned epics, the *Mahābhārata* and the *Ramayana*, which are practical application of the theoretical moral and ethical teaching and life.

In Sanskrit, there are many books which deal purely with moral teaching both in the form of couplet (*Anushtupa Chhand*) and also as simple formula known as *sutra*. In them, the thinkers have presented ways to purify our inner and outer selves and have taught to get success in almost every situation and circumstance, and to lead a peaceful and happy life. They have applied various ways and cited different similes. Some of them have changed the similes into metaphors. They have magical effect and instantly impress the listeners. In almost every congregation, in *panchāyats*, at the time of marriage negotiation and during important sales and purchases, they are quoted vehemently and analysed methodically.

Clarity and easy perception are their qualities that are behind their miraculously long life and popularity. They are so natural that they touch the heart, they are so true that none can deny them. They would not perish till man is alive.

Shukra Niti

We cannot take into consideration the lost treatises, hence we can safely proceed ahead with the most ancient book, solely devoted to moral teaching. It is definitely *Shukra Niti*. That does not mean such teachings are not in the Vedas or the *Upanishads* and in the other branches of the cannon of Sanskrit literature. It simply means that this book has only one aim and it has been composed with only moral teachings as the main subject matter. In most of the other books, the principal subjects are other problems and aspects of life and Universe, but since the morality affects our life and influence our thinking, so moral and ethical teachings came naturally in them. It is not the deliberate subject of that book. While in *Nitishãstras,* the *Niti* is the principal subject, and the only objective behind their creation.

Chãnakya

After that, moral and ethical teachings in *sutras* and *slokas* took shape in Chãnakya who was the son of Rishi Chanak. He wrote all the moral teachings including *Chãnakya Niti* and *Chãnakya Sutra*. He is also called Kautilya and wrote ***Arthashãstra*** under this name. He is famous as the destroyer of Nanda Dynasty and the creator of Maurya Dynasty.

The Science of Ethics (*Nitishãstra*) by Chãnakya has its own value and significance. The importance of *Niti* for the men and gods in India can be gauged with the fact that in *Gita*, Lord Krishna declared: ***nitih asmi jigistãm*** (I'm ethics for those who wish to win).

Chānakya Niti

Chānakya was a great statesman, diplomat and a virtuous man in moral behaviour. He is a special name among the composers of ethical verses for he dedicated all his writing solely to moral teachings and composed nothing else. He had an aim and achieved it. He excelled in every sphere. His teachings are universal and applicable at every place and in any situation. Just by following him, one can easily get worldly success in any field and spiritual solace.

He framed policies with rare prudence, clarity and judiciousness. His *sutras* are still treated as the basis of diplomacy and formation of policies and rules by most of the governments of the world. He is the most popular and most widely read person among the ancient Indian writers.

The following six versions of *Chānakya Niti* are found:

1. ***Vriddha Chānakya I*** – It is the first version and is known as *Sāmānya Vāchanā* (General Version). It has 8 chapters.
2. ***Vriddha Chānakya II*** – It is the second version and is known as *Alankrita Vāchanā* (Ornamental Version) and has 17 chapters. It is named as ***Chānakya Nitidarpan*** with 17 chapters which have 197 *slokas* out of the total available 336. In the easily available versions in the market, all the 336 *slokas* have been included and they

are called either *Chānakya Nitidarpan* or *Chānakya Nitishāstra*.

3. *Chānakya Nitishāstra* – It is the third version and is called *Chānakya Nitishāstra*. In the *Avatarnikā* (Preface), it is claimed that it has been collected from different books and is the seed of all scriptures:

नाना शास्त्र उद्धृतं वक्ष्य राजनीति समुच्चयम्।
सर्वबीजं इदं शास्त्रं चाणक्यं सारसंग्रहं।।

Nānāshāstra udhritam wakshye rājnitisammuchayam
Sarbabeejam idam shāstram Chānakyam sārsangraham

It has been claimed to be the original work of Chānakya which is a proof that it is the most ancient one:

मूलसूत्रं प्रवक्ष्यामि चाणक्येन यथोदितम्।
यस्य विज्ञानमात्रेण मूर्खो भवति पण्डित:।।

Mulashutram prawakshyāmi Chānakyena yathoditam
Yasya vigyānamātrena murkho bhawati panditah

4. *Chānakya Sārsangrah* – It is the fourth version which contains 300 *Anushtupa Britta.* It is divided into three sections and each section contains exactly 100 *slokas*. It teaches not only the politics but also the simple ways of general living. The last couplet lays stress on living in Kāsi (Varanasi) which shows the love of the poet for the place and suggests that either he belonged to Kāsi or had great affinity and respect for the place. So he says that in this mortal world, there are four things

which can be of essence. They are living in Kāsi, truthful living, closeness to Gangā and devotion to Lord Shiva:

असारे खलु संसारे सारमेतत चतुष्टयम्।
काश्यां वासः संगो गंगाम्भः शंभुसेवनम्।।

Asāre khalu samsāre sārametat chatushtayam
Kāsyām bāsah satām sango Gangāmbhah
Shambhusevanam

5. *Laghu Chānakya* – It is divided into 8 chapters and each contains 10 to 13 couplets. It was not available in India but was very popular in European countries for many centuries as it was carried over there by the priests. Perhaps it was first translated in Greek in the year 1825 by Gelenas who was a scholar of Sanskrit.

6. *Chānakya Rājnitishāstra* – It is divided into 8 chapters and contains 534 *slokas* or couplets in Sanskrit. Even this book was not available in India. It was translated in the 9th century AD and was preserved in Tibet. Its verses are also available in the books in China, Mangolia, Manchuria, Java and Bali. But the complete text is available only in Tibet.

Chānakya's *Rājnitishāstra* deals mostly with kings and politics, particularly the 4th and the 5th chapters deal only with the kings, kingdoms, people, policies, diplomacy and other topics related to good and successful governance. In this respect, it is a unique creation which teaches everyone all about emancipation of life, good moral character, happy, smooth and trouble-free life, good governance and the duties of kings, ministers and other government officials so that they can rule well and protect the kingdom from inner revolts and outer attacks.

Even Brihaspati in his *Nitishāstra* has included verses from Chānakya's *Rājnitishāstra*. It is claimed that originally it contained some 1119 *slokas*. In that way, it appears that the total number of the *slokas* composed by Chānakya is more than two thousand.

To many, *Niti Slokas* have greater value but for many, Kautilya's ***Arthashāstra*** is the greatest work. Incidentally, Kautilya means crookedness, cunningness and fraud. Somehow these qualities got associated with Chānakya although he was totally against them; he despised these impurities.

Chānakya Sutras are mostly taken from Kautilya's ***Arthashāstra***. They present the quintessence of Chānakya's views and those of the earlier texts particularly from Brihaspati Niti. On the contrary to the present belief and effort to separate politics and religion, Chānakya held the view that they are inseparable. Chānakya is right because despite raising hue and cry on many occasions, the modern politicians and statesmen have not been able to separate religion from politics. It is this truthfulness and the universality of the truth expressed and theories propounded by those *Sutrakārs* that they are still fresh and useful.

It is our mistake that we are not trying to take benefit from their immense wisdom, and are imbibing materialistic quotations, making these worthless matters the goal of our life.

It is rapidly leading to upheavals and destructions. It is our departure from the moral and ethical teachings of those thinkers that we are unable to stop the crime. Our values are changing and by praising crime and making the criminals a hero, we are sure to change each person into a criminal. We are not thinking as to what will happen to life under universal criminalisation. How can the live bombs and human bombs be checked? Can it be ever stopped?

The climax is that the doctors, who have the responsibility to keep the society healthy, are selling the human organs, and many men have even started eating the human flesh. Hundreds of skeletons are excavated each day with many more still buried inside.

The kids are running away from their homes claiming them to be not worth living yet we are not stopping and taking stock of the situation.

The mind, philosophy, ethics and morality must change if we want life to sustain.

Bhartrihari

Sringārshatakam, Vairāgyashatakam and Nitishatakam

Following the trend created by Vidur and Chānakya, many such books were written but after Chānakya, the *Nitishāstra* takes rest only in Bhartrihari who composed 300 such *slokas* collected in three volumes (100 each) and known as *Sringārshatakam*, *Vairāgyashatakam* and *Nitishatakam*.

Bhartrihari was the most popular poet of his time and with his enchanting verses, he has maintained his popularity since then. He was one thinker who laid equal stress on fate and action. His findings are exquisite and true for all times. In the given verse, he has distinguished men on the basis of fate and action:

प्रारभ्यते न खलु विघ्नभयेन नीचैः।
प्रारभ्य विघ्नविहिता वीरमन्ति मध्याः।।
विघ्नैः पुनःपुनरपि प्रतिहन्यमानः।
प्रारभ्य तु उत्तमजना न परित्यजन्ति।।

Prārbhyate na khalu bighnabhayena nichaih
Prārbhya bighnavihitā biramanti madhyāh
Bighnaih punahpunarapi pratihanyamānāh
Prārbhya tu uttamjanā na parityajanti

(The worst people do not start a work out of the fear that it would not be completed either because they are not lucky or because they would not be doing that hard labour. The men in the middle do start a work but they leave it unfinished when they

face problems. The best do not start a work easily but once they take a start, they finish the work in the face of many problems coming again and again.)

Knowledge and learning was all that Bhartrihari preached. He praised *vidya* in the most balanced way in the following verse:

विद्या नाम नरस्य रूपमधिकम
प्रच्छन्नगुप्तं धनं
विद्या भोगकरी यशः सुखकारी विद्या गुरुणां गुरुः।
विद्या बन्धुजनो विदेशगमने विद्या परा देवता
विद्या राजसु पूज्यते नहि धनं विद्याविहीनः पशुः।।

Vidyā nāma narasya rupamadhikam
prachchhannaguptam dhanam
Vidyā bhogakari yashah sukhakari vidyā gurunām guruh
Vidyā bandhujano videshgamane vidyā parā devtā
Vidyā rājasu pujyate nahi dhanam vidyāvihinah pashuh

(Vidyā or knowledge is the best beauty and greatest decoration of a man. It is his secretly secured wealth. It gives pleasure, fame and all that is needed for a happy life. It is the teacher of teachers. It is revered by kings in place of wealth. Without it, a man is an animal.)

Panchtantra

Panchtantra was translated, perhaps, for the first time in abour 200 BC in Greek after the army of Alexander returned back. Then, it was again translated in 533 AD in Persian by Hakim Burjoi at the behest of Shah Khusro Nausherwan. Since then, it has been translated in almost all the important languages of the world and the scholars from all those languages and literature have tried to write a book like that including Aesop from Greek.

It is called *Panchtantra* because it contains five *tantras.* They are:

- *Mitrabheda*
- *Mitrasamprāpti*
- *Kākolukeeya*
- *Labdhapranāsh*
- *Aparikshitkārkam*

It is the book that made India *Jagadguru* (the World Teacher).

But this fame was declared by Manu himself who explained and established the first ever Human Religion. He wrote clearly in *Manusmriti:*

एतद्देशप्रसूतस्य एकाशादग्रजन्मनः।
स्वं स्वं चरित्रं शिक्षेर्न पृथिव्यां सर्वमानवाः।।

Yetaddeshaprasutasya sakāshādagrajanmanah
Swam swam charitram shiksheran prithivyām sarvamānawāh

(All the men of the world have received interesting and useful teachings from the ancestors of this land of deeds.)

Mitralābha or *Hitopadesh* is direct teaching for general benefit and personal gain.

Nitimanjari is created on the basis of the dialogues of Rig Veda.

Niti Mayukh is another classical book of moral values and ethical teaching.

Dattātreya Nitishāstra or *Awadhuta Gita*, is another great book that gives straightforward teachings:

रागद्वेष विनिर्मुक्तः सर्वभूताहितेरतः।
दृढ़बोधश्च धीरश्च स गच्छेत परमं पदं।।

Rāgadwesh vinirmuktah sarvabhutahite ratah
Dridhbodhashcha dheerashcha sa gachchhet paramam padam

(To be free from attachment, lust, hate and jealousy, to work for the benefit of all living beings, to confidently try to realise the eternal truth, and to have patience are the four steps to the pedestal of bliss and blissful state.)

Truth, non-violence, kindness, forgiveness, help to others, charity and to control the mind are the essence of all Indian moral teachings. Somehow, all the teachings are based on these fundamental needs as a part of our living and thinking.

Kāmāndkeeya Nitisāra was written by Āchārya Kāmandaka in which he has mostly concentrated on kingship, politics, and statesmanship.

Around the time of Buddha, on the pattern of *Panchtantra* many *Granthas* were written in the form of tales, but they were told for ethical and moral teachings. Some such famous books are:

- *Brihatkathā*
- *Vaitālpanchvishati*
- *Brihatkathāmanjari*
- *Boddhisattwāwadāna*
- *Rājatarangani*
- *Vikramcharit*
- *Shukasaptati*
- *Gumāni Niti*
- *Niti Prakāshikā*
- *Nitivākyāmrita*

Later on more books of ethical and moral tales came out which are still very popular. Some important one among them are:

- *Purush Parikshā*
- *Prabandhakosha*
- *Kathāratnākar*
- *Kathāsaritsāgara*
- *Prabandhachintāmani*
- *Dashkumārcharita*
- *Āividhateerthakalp*
- *Bhojaprabandha*

- *Awadānashatak*
- *Divyāvdāna*
- *Bhattakadwātrinshikā*
- *Vividha Teerthakalp*

Purusha Parikshā was composed by the great poet Vidyāpati. People know him only as a poet of Maithili literature but the truth is entirely different. Except *Vidyāpati Padāwali,* all his other 19 works are in Sanskrit. On the basis of his deep knowledge of Sanskrit, he got royal protection. He was a great devotee of both Shiva and Durga. In *Purusha Parikshā* (The Test of a Man) the characteristics of man are presented and tested through moral tales. These are also fables but in place of animals he has taken human beings as characters. The book contains 44 stories which are divided into four chapters as *Veera, Subuddhi, Savidya* and the fourth chapter tests a man on the basis of the four pursuits namely: *Dharma, Artha, Kāma* and *Moksha.*

Some books were written in the form of essays. The following are the important collections of essays:

- *Kritykalptaru*
- *Rājadharmakānda*
- *Rājanitiratnākara*
- *Bhagawant Bhāshkara*
- *Veer Mitrodaya*
- *Smritikaustubha*

Three books by Ādi Shankarāchārya are considered to be the three jewels. They are entertaining and enlightening. They are:

- *Sādhanapanchakam*
- *Dwādashpanchrikā*
- *Charpatapanchrikā*

Shankarāchārya says that man has not as yet realised the instability and mortality of life. He earns wealth and has lust for it. He wishes to get peace from wealth but the sons and relatives behave in such a way that he feels the wastage of life only at the end, and sometimes never. All are aggrieved. They want to control time that waits for none:

अंगं गलितं पलितं मुण्डम दशनवीनिहं जातं तुण्डम।
वृद्धो याति गृहीत्वा दण्डं न मुंचत्याशापिण्डम।।

Angam galitam palitam mundam dashanavihinam jātam tundam
Vriddho yāti gribitwā dandam tadapi na munchtyāshāpindam

(The body becomes weak during the old age, hair grows grey, teeth fall off and one moves with a stick in hand. It is a wonder that despite such doddering condition one wishes to live.)

Along with some original *Sukti-Sangrah* like ***Abhinav Samskrit Subhāsita Shaptashati*** by Āchārya Shrinārāyanā Kānkār, many collections were prepared as

Subhasita-Sangraha. After India got independence, the number of such books has considerably increased.

Kuttanimatta by Dāmodar Gupta is a social satire and aims at improving the life of the people.

Kshemendra's ***Kalā Vilās*** has depicted ten evils: *Dambha, Lobha, Kāma, Veshyāvriti, Kāyathacharita, Mada, Gāyana, Suvarnakārotapatti, Nānā Dhurta* and *Kalā Varnana*. With the help of satire, he has presented healthy teachings.

Although Kshemendra was a poet of the early middle ages but in treatment of his subject he seems to be modern. Kshemendra's ***Darpadalana*** shows the growing ego and its meaninglessness.

Chārucharyā contains hundred *slokas* on general moral living.

Chaturvagra Sangrah describes and teaches the four pursuit of man called *Purushārtha Chatushtaya*.

Samaya Mātrikā, an original book on prostitutes, teaches how to save oneself from their deadly net.

Deshopadesha and ***Narmamāla*** are humorous satires.

The following are some other important books:

(i) ***Vairāgya Shataka*** by Appyaya Dikshit

(ii) ***Lokokti Muktāwali*** by Dakshināmurti

(iii) ***Drishtānta Kalikā Shatama*** by Kusumdeo

(iv) ***Kalividambana*** by Neelkatha Dikshit

(v) *Mugdhopadesh* by Jalahana

(vi) *Prabodha Sudhākar* by Shankarāchārya

(vii) *Shānti hataka* by Shilahana

(viii) *Bhāva Vilās* by Rudrakavi

(ix) *Anyokti Shataka* by Vireswar

(x) *Anyāpadesh Shataka* by Neelkantha Dikshit

(xi) *Sabhāranjana* by Neelkantha Dikshit

(xii) *Subhāshit Ratnakosha* by Vidyādhar Pandit

(xiii) *Saduktikarnāmrita* by Shridhar Dāsa

(xiv) *Sukti Muktāwali* by Jalahana

(xv) *Subhāshitāwali* by Ballabhadeo

(xvi) *Padyāmrita Tarangani* by Hari Bhāskara

(xvii) *Padya Rachanā* by Ankolkar

(xviii) *Vidyādhar Sahastrakāra* by Vidyākara Mishra

Moral Values in Scriptures

Indian literature is full of moral and ethical tales. They courageously and clearly face the question: Is it "Art for Art's sake" or "Art for the sake of life"? It means whether literature was to be produced just for pleasure or whether there should be some obvious purpose behind the creation. The Indians wisely and in a determined way accepted that there must be a purpose behind every creation. Their vision is always crystal clear. They know their preferences and follow them meticulously well. Even the poisonous snakes were created with a divine and healthy purpose to breathe in and suck out the poison from the atmosphere. We have unknowingly killed all the snakes. As a result, the poison in the atmosphere is increasing fast and we are always adding some more poison to it. There is a purpose behind everything. Similarly a purpose was accepted as essential behind every work of art or literature. Hence, the completely aesthetic and purely poetic creations are rich in music and give immense pleasure. Thus, they too serve a definite purpose. The acceptance of purpose in writing and artistic creation gave meaning and essence to the dedicated labour of the learned and not so learned ancient and modern writers and artists of India. This purpose is always behind the creation of ethical and moral tales, couplets, quadruplets, poems, songs and treatises in each local, regional and national language.

Some scheming mind must have been behind the loss of books on the one side and loss of its importance on the other side. What was known as *Nitishāstra* was replaced by *Kāntā Sammat Upadesh* which aimed at tenderness and touched the readers smoothly.

The whole *Niti-Wāngamaya* was included under the head of poetry. It was composed in metre but it was not poetry in the regular sense of the word, and it was never mild like the sensual whispering. As a result, it lost its importance and today, Indians are not realising what a grand and precious wealth is lying there unused and uncared for. The basic problem with the modern Indians is that neither they know nor they are sincerely trying to know the incomparable richness of both our remote and immediate past.

These ethical teachings have laid stress on two great principles of humility and good moral character. The humble with good moral character grow and help others grow. Howsoever learned a man may become, but if he lacks humility and good moral character then he is ignorant and living in utter darkness.

One must do away with anger, ego and pride. The Sanskrit equivalent of humble is *nama* which is a quality that leads to *namana* (salute).

Nama, namratā and *namana* are great qualities. That person cannot fail who possesses these qualities. In this context, two *slokas* from the *Mahābhārata* (*Vana Parva* 28:31 and *Udyoga Parva* 34:48) are being quoted here:

मृदुना दारुणं हन्ति मृदुना हन्त्यादारुणं।
नासाध्यं मृदुना किंचित तस्मात तीव्रतरं मृदु॥

Mridunā dārunam hanti mridunā hantyadārunam
Nāsādhyam mridunā kinchit tasmāt tibrataram mridu

(Humility destroys the rigidity, humility, wins humility; there is nothing beyond the power of humility; so humility is the best possible way.)

शीलं प्रधानं पुरुषे तद् यस्येहा प्रणस्यतिः।
ता तस्य जीवितेनार्थो न धनेन न बन्धुभिः।।

Sheelam pradhānam purushe tad yasyeha pranashyati
Ta tasya jeevitenārtho na dhanena na bandhubhih

(Good moral charcter is the most important thing in life. He, who has lost his charcter, has nothing left in life — no wealth, no relative, no friend.)

What Suniti taught her son Dhruva in *Vishnu Purāna* (1:11:24) is a lesson we must all learn and teach the posterity:

सुशीलो भव धर्मात्मा मैत्रः प्रनिहितेरातः।
निम्नं तथापः प्रवनाः पात्रमायन्ति सम्पदः।।

Sushilo bhawa dharmātmā maitrah prānihiteratah
Nimanam tathāpah prawanāh pātramāyānti sampadah

(Be a man of good character, humble and virtuous, do good to all living beings like a lowland where water easily gets collected, and be such a good and able container so that the wealth can remain in you.)

These moral teachings are enchanting and illuminating. They have the power to mould, modulate and metamorphose a stressful life into a healthy, happy and hunger-free serene and sublime life which the modern men are vying to get it but have no idea how to get and from where to get it?

The thinkers have used both the direct and indirect methods to impart proper lessons to mankind. In direct method, all the mistakes, wrong notions, right ideas, lapses in character, deeds or thinking are presented directly, along with the suggestions of do's and don'ts. In the indirect method, symbol, simile, metaphor, satire, irony and humour are used to present the same things which take off the hard and biting truth from it and lessen the total and final effect.

Yet another fact must be mentioned that some sponsored writing also came towards the end of the middle ages to make a mockery of life and wealth of ancient India. It is really very sad that most of the writings of the last few centuries come directly from that sponsored field. On many occasions, many questions were raised whenever the works abusing India and Indianness were amply awarded. This has misled many generations who have developed a liking for everything non-Indian. At every step, the Indians are considered to be losers and as such they have been living under strain.

They are desperately searching a way out but they are not searching for the answers in the scriptures or in the *Nitishāstra* which is an integral part of the scriptures and can easily transform the life into a healthy and happy one. Once they find the true answer here, the roar, the craving and the agony will come abruptly to an end.

Both the *Niti Sutras* and *Niti Slokas* are very simple to understand and easy to follow. One needs just purity and determination of mind.

○○

7

Grantha-Trai — The Quintessence of Hindu Scriptures

The three great scriptures — the *Rāmāyana*, the *Mahābhārata* and *Srimad Bhāgwat Mahāpurana* are known as the *grantha-trai*. The first two are famous as epics while the third one is known as a *Purāna*. The Hindus know them to be poetic and admit the excellence of the verses but they accept, talk and revere them as their scriptures. The poetic qualities are often discussed but thousands of other valuable thoughts and teachings get importance because they have direct bearing and impact on the lives of the billions of Hindus. Moreover, there are numerous other great epics which have least religious values and hence they are mostly discussed as literary works for the instant pleasure that they give: *sadyah parnirbirtaye*.

The *grantha-trai* is the quintessence of *Hindu scriptures*. What we know about or say Hinduism to be, is based on these three precious works. They are poetic narratives and enjoy all the benefits of stories and tales. Each of them is a unified whole and each of them has numerous short tales. Direct teachings as well as teachings through words and deeds are present in them. They contain what and why the gods preach and do something, why they punish and why they shower blessings and boons. They show the depth in the relations and the way they maintain them and also the rescue acts. Everything, including the promises, blessings and the curses, is important. These books are the physical presentation of all that the incarnations stood for. In essence, they are the same. However on the basis of the way the ideas have been presented, the *Rāmāyana* is treated as an epic, the *Mahābhārata* as history and Srimad Bhāgwat as a *Purāna*. They have also been termed as '*Upjivya-kāvya*'. The *Rāmāyana* is action-oriented, the *Mahābhārata* shows practical struggle for existence and *Srimad Bhāgwat* deals with general feelings.

Padmashri Baldev Upadhyaya has discussed *Srimad Bhāgwat Mahāpurāna* as an epic and has pointed out its poetic qualities. Yet it has remained the most famous and accepted scripture for the Hindus. It is equally powerful in the *grantha*-trinity.

Grantha-trai is widely read and is the most discussed scripture in enchanting narrative form. *Grantha-trai* contains everything that Hinduism stands for, boasts of and all that the Hindus follow. They are the most authentic representatives of the Hindu scriptures. In other words, what the Hindus follow and accept are there in these *Granthas*. That is the basic and the most important reason that whenever we ask a Hindu, "What are your scriptures?", he mentions these three books only. Most of them might not be able to recall the name of a fourth one. As the fourth book, they invariably mention *Srimad Bhagwad Gita*. They hardly realise that it is a part of the *Mahābhārata*. When reminded of, they will readily accept it.

It is a fact that most of the Hindus have not read these holy books, but they all know what is there in them. The system of teaching in Hindu families and society is so rich and perfect, strong and interwoven that they are taught whatever needed in a very subtle and easy way. They seldom realise that they are being given lessons in religion or taught religious books or being baptised. It can be safely said that these three books contain and represent all the central ideas and philosophy of Indian life and culture. That Indian life and culture has adopted all that has been presented in and through these books of the highest religious values. It is pertinent here to quote a widely quoted statement, "That which is in this epic is elsewhere too but that which is not in the *Mahābhārata* is nowhere else":

धर्मे अर्थे च कामे च मोक्षे च भरतर्षभ।
यदिहास्ति तदन्यत्र यन्नेहास्ति न तत् क्वचित्।।

Dharma hyarthe cha kāme cha mokshe cha bharatarshabha
Yadihāsti tadanyatra yananahāsti na tat kwachit

The real reason behind their immense popularity is their recital, known as *pravachans*, by *pandits* and experts who tell the devotional story. The effect on the audience is magical. The audience feels absorbed in it. They feel to be a part of the story. From time immemorial, till some 30 years back, *'Bhāgwatkathāvāchan'* was performed for around nine months except the wet months of rainy seasons. Now, the construction of halls and auditoriums in every part of the country provides facilities for religious congregations and has ensured that the *Bhāgwatkathā* will be told, analysed and discussed throughout the year in the presence of huge gatherings. At present, *Bhāgwatkathā* is told throughout the year.

On the other hand, in thousands of district headquarters, the *Rāmāyana* or *Rāmacharita Mānas* is recited, worshipped and discussed every year during *Chait Rāmanavami* and other months. The recitation and narration of the *Mahābhārata* is arranged at only selected places and continues for months till it is finished. That is the way Hindu Religion is taught to the masses. In turn they discuss among themselves and whenever there is some question or problem, the local people arrange single (24 hours) or double (48 hours) *asthayām*. Along with the singers of devotional songs, some learned men are invited who make everything clear in their own way.

Teachings of Grantha-Trai

All the three epics, in their own right teach everything that a common man should know and follow. The aim has been achieved in the most convincing and captivating manner. That is the reason why they enjoy universal acceptance and reverence. They are also known as ***Ārsh-kāvya.*** The Hindus analyse, discuss and compare their scriptures from different angles, points of view and social setup. The various statements, changes, external or internal differences are all put to test on different touchstones and all those statements and incidents in themselves are treated as touchstones. They do not criticise them but the discussions and analysis are so open and divergent that they give the illusion of deliberate and prejudiced criticism. This approach has kept the Hindus alive for they have adjusted themselves well with the changing milieu and have always been alive to the surrounding. In congregations and by discussions, they always come to positive conclusions and choose the best path for leading their personal growth and a better life. They have correctly and consciously adopted *'yug-dharma'*, the religion of the age, for dealing with the crisis in any age and time. With subtle variations, the numerous ways shown by our forefathers give us options and keep all the doors open for us. One can follow any path provided one does everything for humanity and with pious intentions. They have given eternal values for a changing society. They have treated the whole world as a single nest — *vishwam ekam needam.*

The mass appeal depends mostly on the teachings (percept and example) given by Rãma or Krishna. The Hindus accept and worship one without denying or denouncing the other. There is no conflict between Rãma and Krishna. The subtle inclusion of the *Rãmãyana* in the *Mahãbhãrata* is the height of such assimilation. Numerous books were written down the ages on the themes of these three books. One thousand *Rãmãyanas* are available only in Kannada. After the popularity of printing press, lakhs of books are published dealing with different characters or incidents or parts of these three books. It will be a futile effort either to count them or to make a chronological list of such books. They are deeply rooted in the life and mind of the Indians. Naturally Grierson claimed that *Rãmacharita Mãnas* is more popular in the Himalayan Valley than the *Bible.*

The *rishis* and saints, saint-poets and saint-singers very wisely and aptly and at appropriate places left the options open for the masses or for an individual to opt for a way and to choose their Lord for worshipping. All the ways and doors are open to them and they are free to adopt any of them. It is the piety and inner growth that has been given value. That is the only thing needed for salvation. At times, mostly in *stutis* the benefits of worshipping a particular God at a particular time or in a particular way is categorically given:

Ye pathanti narã bhaktyã teshãm shambhu prasidati

Srimad Bhãgwat Mahãpurãna

Benefits of these scriptures have alluring effect on the mind of both the devotees and common man. They have a lot to do with the immense popularity and mass acceptance of these three scriptures. Let us see some of them from *Srimad Bhãgwat Mahãpurãna*:

नित्यं भागवतम् पुराणं पठेत नरः।
प्रत्येकक्षरं भवेतस्य कपिलादानजम् फलम्।।

Nityam bhãgwatam purãnam pathate narah
Pratyaksharam bhawetasya kapilãdãnajam phalam

(The man who reads the Bhãgwat Purãna every day gets the benediction of the donation of a kapilã (all giving) cow for each letter that he pronounces.)

श्लोकार्धं श्लोकपादं वा नित्यं भागवतोद्भवं।
पठते श्रिनुयाद यस्तु गोसहस्त्र फलं लभेत।।

Slokãrdham slokapãdam wa nityam bhãgwatodbhawam
Pathate shrinuyãd yastu gosahastra phalam labheta

(He who recites half or quarter sloka gets the benefit of the donation of one thousand cows.)

यः पठेत प्रयतो नित्यम श्लोकम् भागवतम् सुत।
अष्टादशपुराणानां फलमाप्नोति मानवः।।

Yah patheta prayato nityam slokam bhāgwatam suta
Astadaspurānānām phalamāpnoti mānawah

(He who reads with piety and dedication one sloka of Bhāgwat every day gets the benefit of reading the 18 Purānas.)

Such announcements and immaculate narrative technique has resulted into its complete acceptance by all. Its words or teachings have never been questioned.

Srimad Bhāgwat Purāna at a later stage became *Srimad Bhāgwat Mahāpurāna* when the saints declared and the people accepted it as the holy book that holds the essence of all scriptures expressed and explained through the story of Lord Krishna.

Srimad Bhāgwat Mahāpurāna is treated as the '*Kalpvriksha*', the tree which gives everything and fulfils all the desires and wishes. It frees and keeps one away from hurdles, problems, troubles and dangers. It increases knowledge, detachment and devotion.

Nine types of devotions have been preached in *Srimad Bhāgwat Mahāpurāna* which widens the scope and allows a lot of free thinking and movements. It is known as '*nawadhā bhakti*':

श्रवणं कीर्तनं विष्णोह स्मरणं पादसेवनम्।
अर्चनं वंदनं दास्यं सख्यमात्मनिवेदनम्।।

Shravanam kirtanam vishnoh smaranam pādsevanam
Archanam vandanam dāsyam sakhyamātmanivedanam
[i. *Shravan* (listening to the Name) ii. *Kirtan* (to recite the Name) iii. *Smaranam* (to remember the Lord) iv. *Pād sevanam* (serving the Lord) v. *Archanā* (to worship the Lord) vi. *Vandanam* (to salute the Lord) vii. *Dāsya* (as a servant) viii. *Sakhya* (as a friend) ix. *Ātma Nivedanam* (to request the Lord).]

Two other forms ***prem lakshanā*** and ***parā bhakti*** are also added to it: to make it 11.

Even one out of these ways will give solace and satisfaction, closeness and intimacy, fullness and richness, which will keep one charged with energy and emotion. *Srimad Bhāgwat's* advice to all is clear and open that all of us should seek the closeness of the Lord.

The propogation of all the common ways by *Srimad Bhāgwat Mahāpurāna* resulted into instant success and fame. Moreover, it has always been closer to the sentiments of the general masses. Its musical quality is also behind its immense popularity and general acceptance.

Srimad Bhāgwat Mahāpurāna is a touchstone for scholars. It presents the essence of the *Shrutis* in condensed form. It gives an authentic conclusion to the *Mahābhārata*. It is an exposition as well as a commentary on the *Brahma Sutra*. At various places, the famous *mantras* of *Shrutis* have been quoted with minor changes and alterations. Its poetry and music has some magical qualities which have so far kept intact the interest of the readers down the ages. The whole of the *Dasam skandh* (10th Chapter) is known for its emotions and passion (in *Venu-geet*, *Gopi-geet*, *Yugal-geet* and *Mahishi-geet*). Many people spend their whole life in this chapter alone and fail to enjoy many other spiritual things.

The Rãmãyana

The *Rãmãyana* is the oldest among the *Grantha-trai* and Maharshi Valmiki who composed it is known as the first poet. It is known as '*chaturvinshati sãhastri samhitã*' because it contains twenty four thousand *slokas*. In other words, there are one thousand *slokas* for each letter in the *Gãyatri Mantra*. The first letter of each of the thousand slokas begins with a letter from *Gãyatri* and thus completes the *Gãyatri Mantra*.

The *Rãmãyana* is the most ancient and the basic scripture of the Hindus, though it is an epic. It is not the poetry or the poetic quality that is important but it is the faith of the people and the presentation of the protagonist as the perfect man who in turn is an incarnation of Lord Vishnu. The Hindus have faith in Rãma, more than in anyone else. It hardly makes any difference to them whether that Rãma has been depicted by Vãlmiki or Tulsi or Kesava or Kãlidãs. It explains and elucidates Vaishanva philosophy and that is enough for the Hindus who easily and completely surrender to their Lords: Brahma or Shiva or Vishnu in all his nine incarnations. Again it is a matter of faith. The Hindus possess a lot of faith.

The *Rāmāyana* is definitely timeless. For that matter all the writings on Sri Rāma are treated as sacred and Rāma is universal. The *Rāmāyana* transcends all time and space. Rāma is not for one but for all. He is a living and dynamic emblem of all the ideals. He presents before the humanity a moral standard and sublime social and personal relation. He does everything right. He has both the reward and punishment. Both his anger and pleasure are permanent. He would not spare a criminal who should be killed and his eyes would never redden at the sight of the one who is innocent:

नास्य क्रोधः प्रसादो वा निरर्थोऽस्ति कदाचन।
हन्त्येष नियमाद् वध्यानवध्येषु न कुप्यति।।

Nāsya krodhah pramādo wā nirarthoasti kadāchana
Hantyesh niyamād vadhyānavadhyeshu na kupyati

Rāma is the reason that this book and many other epics or other creations on Rāma are not restricted to one age. They are for all ages. They depict the ideals and elements of permanent value. All the characters are the representatives of some characteristics, some trends and ideals. 'Sublimity' is the word that characterises the whole book. It easily and powerfully establishes truth, morality and beauty: *satyam, shivam* and *sundaram*. It is the character that makes one a God, man or devil.

The Mahābhārata

The aim and object behind the composition of the *Mahābhārata* is never to describe the war or the internal struggle but complete disarmament and mortality in life, so that men can live in peace and help each other. Naturally, the overall tone throughout the book is that of peace and not war. *Gita*, an integral part of this great epic is a concise treatise on the way we should lead our life by following the principles described in it. But two things are of immense value. One is the declaration that man has control only on his deeds. He should work and forget about the result. If the work has been done well with all needed piety, the result is bound to be good. And the most important thing is that if one is a detached devotee, then rest of the things will be taken care of by the God.

The *Mahābhārata* is a great epic in every sense of the word. It is divided in 18 parts which are called '*Parvas*'. It includes some other great stories. They are:

i. *Shakuntalopākhyāna*

ii. *Matasyopākhyāna*

iii. *Rāmopākhyāna*

iv. *Shivi Upākhyāna*

v. *Savitri Upākhyāna*

vi. *Nalopākhyāna*

Ved Vyās has himself claimed that without knowing the *Mahābhārata* one cannot get complete knowledge.

Yo vidyāchchaturo vedān sāngopanishado dwijah
Na chākhyānamidam vidyānnaiva sa syādwichakshanah

— *Ādi Parva* (2:28)

It is so because in his eyes the *Mahābhārata* is economics, scripture and the art of lovemaking:

अर्थशास्त्रमिदं प्रोक्तं धर्मशास्त्रमिदं महत्।
कामशास्त्रमिदं प्रोक्तं व्यासेनामितुबुद्धिना।।

Arthashāstramidam proktam dharmashāstramidam mahat
Kāmshāstramidam proktam vyāsenāmitubuddhinā

— *Ādi Parva* (2:83)

He, who has heard this mellifluous juicy tale will get no sap from other tales as after listening to the lilting sound of the cuckoo one will not appreciate the cacophonous sound of a crow:

श्रुत्वा त्विद्मुपाख्यानम् श्राव्यमन्यन रोचते।
पुंसकोकिलगिरं श्रुत्वा रुक्षादवान्क्षस्य वागीव।।

Shrutwā twidmupākhyānam shrāvyamanyana rochate
Punskokilgiram shrutwā rukshādhwānkshashya wāgiva

— *Ādi Parva* (2:84)

It includes the ethics and moral teachings a complete Vidur, Bhishma and others. That is why it is of epic. From the very beginning, it has been accepted as a Scripture. It is a representative book of religion. For men, it is full of teachings in sweet and metrical composition. Ved Vyās has emphasised the point that one should never set religion aside despite carnal appetite, fear or lust because religion is eternal:

न जातु कामान्न भयान्न लोभाद धर्मं त्यजेजीवितस्यापि हेतोः।
धर्मो नित्यः सच दुःखे त्वनित्ये जीवो हेतुर्स्य त्वनित्यः।।

Na jātu kāmānna bhayānna lobhād Dharmam tyajejiwitasyāpi hetoh
Dharmo nityah such-dukhe twanitye Jeevo nityo heturasya twanityah

The *grantha-trai,* the *Rāmāyana*, the *Mahābhārata* and *Srimad Bhāgwat Mahāpurāna,* are life and history of Hindus. It is no wonder that they are the religion and the scriptures. They represent the Hindus and the Hindus live by them. They are their real strength, courage, purity and the cause behind their steady development, sustenance and humanism.

The Gita

Bhagwad Gita is popularly known as the *Gita* or the Divine Song. It is universally regarded as one of the basic scriptures and held in high esteem by philosophers, theists, and ethical teachers both of ancient and modern times. The *Gita* tries to synthesise and reconcile all views and all paths. It teaches that God, while transcending all, also manifests Himself in life in diverse forms. There are different ways of realising Him:

- Through Knowledge (*Jnāna Yoga*)
- Through Devotion (*Bhakti Yoga*)
- Through action without attachment (*Nishkāma Karma Yoga*)

Any of these can be chosen, according to one's own liking and ability or fitness. The duties prescribed in all the paths are equally sacred. There should be no conflict among different faiths and paths. There are natural divisions among men in accordance with their intrinsic qualities: *sat*, *raj* or *tam,* and according to their action. The capacities and duties of men vary according to these qualities and not according to their hereditary staus.

Yoga in the Gitā

1: ॐ

The Gitā, the most ancient and sacred book of yoga,
Deals mainly with only two fundamental kinds of yoga,
That has been mixed and remixed in various ways,
And finally, it is subdivided into eighteen kinds of yoga.

2: ॐ

The two main kinds of yoga are the toughest *Sankhya Yoga*,
And basic, the easier and appropriate *Niskāma Karma Yoga*,
The whole humanity has been declared hold and right on it,
To understand, analyse, adapt and follow essential yoga.

3: ॐ

The *Gitā* defines yoga as detachment and equanimity,
As an act of balancing and centring the infinity,
As an inspiration to transcend ego into pure self,
And getting rare super consciousness and divinity.

4: ॐ

Yoga helps deepest awareness to the point of liberation,
With intuition, wisdom and experience getting salvation,
It develops natural ways to access to cosmic energy,
And it directs the inner energy to healthy fruition.

5: ॐ

Sankhya Yoga defines categories of mortal existence,
Where individual constitution, *Prakriti*, gets substance,
It is striving for getting united to the Eternal *Purusha*,
Till then it remains pure and conscious insistence.

6: ॐ

Until it gets access to divine pure consciousness,
That is known as the *Purusha*, extreme awareness,
It is an effort to experience the purest blissful state,
That is known as *Moksha*, liberation, egolessness.

7: ॐ

Yogis break, get freedom from mundane acts,
From old habits, lifeless patterns and deadly pacts,
They shake off the anxiety of past and future,
And swim smoothly in the stream of present facts.

8: ॐ

Yoga helps in achieving a balance in Time and Space,
Where present glows, past and present have no trace,
They become a part of the intuitive personal experience,
Enable to see events clearly, adding glamour and grace.

9: ॐ

Each moment offers an opportunity to become purer,
Delicately and deliberately moving on selected paths fewer,
Then whatever comes is endured courageously well,
Physique stronger, mind sterner, self becomes demurer.

10: ॐ

The individual constitution *Prakriti* becomes a tool,
To strive to become sublime, remain sane and cool,
Till it gets access to *Purusha,* Divine True Consciousness,
For Joining *Prakriti* and *Purusha* the body works as a pool.

11: ॐ

The *Gitā* makes clear that yoga means to be active till alive,
Not to leave the evil free but at it with all might to strike,
We have no control over coming moments, events to happen,
Without thinking and expecting results, we must sincerely strive.

(From *Yoga in Spiritual Quadruplets*)

The teachings of the *Gitā* have been an inspiration to Indian social and religious faiths and reformation down the ages, and the faith in it has grown deep in the modern era when the modern reformers and political leaders who usually remain engaged in fighting artificial social inequalities trying to harmonise different religions started correcting these evils with the help of the highest ideal of the *Gitā* — work without attachment.

The Contents of the Gitã

Chapters/Shlokas	Subject
1st/1-27	*Arjuna-Vishãda-Yoga: Warriors counted, conch-sound, inspection of armies*
1st/28-47	*Weakness, compassion and grief of Arjuna*
2nd/1-30	*Sãnkhya-Yoga: Weaknesses discussed, Sãnkhya Yoga, a warrior needs to fight*
2nd/31-72	*Niskãma Karma-Yoga: Characteristics and achievements of a person who has stability in mind*
3rd/1-24	*Karma-Yoga: Work with detachment, needs of Yaga, wisemen and God too need to work*
3rd/25-43	*Characteristics of wise and ignorant, work without lust or desire*
4th/1-23	*Jnãna-Karma-Sanyãsa-Yoga: importance of God with qualities; conduct of great yogis*
4th/24-42	*Yajna discussed separately with results, importance of knowledge and wisdom*
5th/1-12	*Karma-Sanyãsa-Yoga: Sãnkhya and Nishkãma discussed, characteristics and importance*
5th/13-29	*Jnãna-Yoga: description of meditation with devotion*

6th/1-32	*Atma-Sanyama-Yoga: Niskāma-Karma and Yogarudh Purush, encouraging for salvation*
6th/33-47	*Controlling mind, what happens to a fallen yogi*
7th/1-19	*Jnāna-Vigyāna-Yoga, God pervades all as cause*
7th/20-30	*Praise to them who know the effect and form of God*
8th/1-7	*Akshar-Brahman-Yoga: Arjuna's 7 Questions and answers*
8th/8-28	*The subject/object of Bhakti-Yoga and that of Shukla and Krishna Path*
9th/1-15	*Rāja-Vidya-Rāja-Guhya-Yoga: subject of knowledge, creation of the Universe*
9th/16-34	*Virtuous versus Demons: form of God, final outcome of detached and attached devotion, former praised*
10th/1-11	*Bibhuti Yoga: God has no beginning and no end, benefits of knowing God, Yoga Shakti, Bhakti Yoga*
10th/12-42	*Arjuna requests to describe Yoga Shakti, Krishna tells all about the Powers and Yoga Shakti*

11th/1-31	*Viswarupa-Darshan-Yoga: Cosmic Self, Sanjay describes it; Arjuna worships and praises Cosmic Self*
11th/32-55	*Krishna shows his Chaturbhuj rupa and Soumya rupa*
12th/1-12	*Bhakti-Yoga: better of the two devotees of God with qualities and God without qualities, the ways to get revelation*
12th/13-20	*Characteristics of the person who has achieved union with God*
13th/1-18	*Kshetra-Kshetragya-Vibhāga Yoga: its object with knowledge*
13th/19-34	*The detail of Prakriti and Purush*
14th/1-18	*Gunatrai-Vibhāga-Yoga: Creation of the Universe through Prakriti and Purush, details of three qualities — Satoguna, Rajoguna and Tamoguna*
14th/19-27	*The characteristics of a person above and over qualities*
15th/1-11	*Purushottama Yoga: Universe as a tree and all about the living being*
15th/12-20	*Influence and form of God and Kshar-Akshar Purush*

16th/1-20	*Daivāsur-Sampati Vibhāga-Yoga: Divine and Demonic wealth with outcome, characteristics of Demonic wealth and the resultant fall*
16th/21-24	*Encouragement to forsake deeds against the scriptures and to adopt deeds advised by it*
17th/1-6	*Shraddhātrai-Vibhāga-Yoga: Penance against scriptures; divisions of āhāra, yajna and tapa*
17th/7-28	*Use of 'Aum Tatsat' explained*
18th/1-48	*Moksha-Sanyāsa-Yoga: Tyāga — Karma and the theory of Sānkhya, Divisions of Jnāna, Karma, Kartā, Buddhi and Dhriti according to Gunatrai, Varna-Dharma along with its outcome*
18th/49-78	*Devotion to knowledge, description of Niskāma Karma Yoga along with Devotion, Hari Aum Tatsat*

OO

8

Hindus and Scriptures

मंगलं भगवान् विष्णु मंगलं गरुणध्वज,
मंगलं पुण्डरीकाक्षं मंगलाय तनोऽहरि।

Mangalam bhagwān Vishnu mangalam garuradhwaja
Mangalam pundarikāksham mangalāya tanohari

Hindus are different

Everything religious, from written tradition to oral expression, is scripture. Everything written or said in Sanskrit is scripture. Everything associated with gods, demi-gods, sages, saints, *munis*, *āchrāryas* and *pandits* is scripture. For them, Vedas are there in the words of the *Brahman*. So, the Vedas, *Shrutis*, *Smritis*, *Purānas*, *Upanishads*, *Kabir Vani*, *Sant Vani*, wise sayings are all scriptures. It makes no difference whether they are in Pāli, Upbhransh, Awadhi, Maithili, Bengali or in any other local dialect. *Hanumān Chālisa*, *Shiva Chālisa*, *Ganesh Stuti* or *Shiva Mahimna Strota* are as great as *Durgāsaptshati* or *Vishnu Sahastranām*. They hardly care whether they know all the one thousand names of

Lord Vishnu or not but it is enough for them that he has so many names. In that way, the name hardly matters. It is the depth of their personal dedication that is important. If it gives wisdom and peace and promises release from the endless cycle of birth and death, then it is a scripture. For them, he is an ignorant person who cannot recite *Hanumān Chālisa* or the *ārati* of the Eternal Mother.

The Hindus are different because it is very difficult to say what is important for them and what is not. For some Hindus, one festival holds a great value and for the rest, some other festival might be more insignificant. One will opt for Onam, the other for Pongal, one for Lakshmi Puja, and yet another for Ganesh Puja and so on. It can happen even among the members of a single family or one religion. Because of this apparent difference, most of the people feel that the Hindus are a divided lot. It is never so. In the matter of religion, devotion and dedication, they are all one. The *rishis* are behind such oneness. Hindus believe that they are the direct descendents of *rishis.* The *rishis* are the original forefathers. The *rishis* provide the all-important *Gotra* of Hindus. The Hindus know their *Gotra* by the name of the *rishi* whose offspring they are. They have carried over that name for millenniums from time immemorial and are ready to carry it over to the eternity. They cannot do away with their *Gotra*. *Gotra* is not needed daily but usually at the time of marriage it gains importance. The *Gotra* is asked for matchmaking. Now the crux of the matter is that the people of same *Gotra*, whether Shudra or Vaishya or Kshatriya or Brahmin, are brothers, for they are the sons of the same *rishi*. This *Gotra* has a lot to do with DNA. Even from modern scientific viewpoint, the faith and adherence to this custom seems quite authentic.

The Hindus are different because they have a positive outlook and assertive nature. They seldom deny. On the contrary, they accept all. They hardly feel any practical difference or problem in *Saguna* and *Nirguna*. Both are the same for them. Both are their Almighty God. All known incarnations are gods for them. All are gods; from the Trinity to Aum to Swastik, from Ganesh to Nārad to Nandi, from Garuda to Hanumān, all are gods to them. They have a god of their personal liking, a family god, a village deity, a separate god for each *puja* or *yajna*, a separate god for each day, each month, year, decade, plantation, harvest, birth, life, success, failure, death. On a rough estimate, they have 33,000 gods, goddesses, and deities. And the wonder is that they are not polytheists!

The Hindus are different as they believe in One God without denying others. During their *puja* they follow a wonderful philosophy. Pandit Hazari Prasad Dwivedi was the first to draw our attention towards this philosophy.

At the time of the rites, rituals, worship, they take one main god and the others are accepted to be subordinate to that Almighty. At another place or time, the sequence can change. In this way, each god can be worshipped after any other. It is Henotheism. It is neither Monotheism nor Polytheism.

The Hindus are different for each one is a theist as well as an atheist. Each Hindu worships the *Brahman* without qualities of an incarnation. He feels no complexities and has no dilemma. His dilemma is illusion, the *Māyā*, and he tries hard to get rid of her.

The Hindus are different. They may not be able to read but they will present scriptures as sacred offerings to those who can read, mostly to *pandits* and declare such offerings as the best. For them, it is as good as reading and knowing them.

The Hindus are different as they can worship on any day, at any place, any time and any God and claim that if there is purity at heart then nothing else has any value (*man changā toh kathauti mein Ganga*). On the other hand, they may consult a *pandit*, get a date, time, place, god fixed and claim that there cannot be purity without *hawan*. They are all open-minded. They look at life in a wider perspective. They can easily live in the cosmic self. They are both the *anu* (atom) and *brahmānd* (Cosmos) and claim *Aham Brahmāsmi*.

The Hindus are different for they believe that their *Shāstras* are their *pandit, pothi* and *patras*. What is written in the *patra* is the Absolute Truth. One word printed in the *patra* is a very small letter '*kumbha*' or '*ardhakumbha*'. Millions of people throng at Prayāg for ritual bath during the Kumbha Mela. Hinduism is wonderful and the Hindus are simply amazing. They may indulge in hot debates with the *pandits* but they will still obey and follow them. The excerpts from the *Purānas* and *Smritis* are the most important scriptures for them, yet all their rituals are performed on the basis of those *pothis*. They are like booklets, but they are the most revered scriptures. They are hundreds in number. A few of them are:

1. *Sri Satyanārāyanvratkathā*
2. *Durgasaptshati*
3. *Saraswatipujapaddhati*
4. *Lakshmipujanvidhi*
5. *Lakhraopujanpaddhati*
6. *Vivāhpaddhati*
7. *Janmsanskārpaddhati*
8. *Sri Ganeshpujanvidhi*
9. *Karmabipāksamhita*
10. *Shrāddhapaddhati*
11. *Dainik Āchārvidhi*
12. *Nityakarmapaddhati*

13. *Kuberpujan*
14. *Shāligrāmpujan*
15. *Haritālikāvrat Kathā*
16. *Navagrahpujan*
17. *Pārthivapujan*
18. *Pitritarpanvidhi*

All these books are in Sanskrit. They form the base of every religious ritual. People do not understand it but they know that all the sacred mantras must be recited in Sanskrit, and that is all. In this way, Sanskrit is very much alive and active in every Hindu home and temple. People may claim it to be a dead language but it is not. It may not be able to give job in public or private sector but it can keep millions engaged on its own. There is no other language in the world which gives wisdom to so many persons all on its own. We can live without Hindi or English but we cannot live without Sanskrit because of these numerous scriptures.

The Hindus are different for they are the incarnations of faith, hope, devotion, tolerance, contentment, and everything positive and human. Just by oral tradition, they know the scriptures and have grasped them so well that they will place irrefutable logic based on them or the epics or the sayings of the saints. They will resign to fate and keep on working steadily and incessantly without expecting anything.

Jāhi bidhi rākhe Rām, tāhi vidhi rahiye

(Live as the God wishes, or secretly directs you to live).

They may not have even seen the *Gitã* but they know the *Gitã* and follow it, truly and honestly. They honestly believe in the proverb "Man proposes, God disposes." They have no complaint. They have a common belief 'It was written in fate' or 'It was not in fate'. It is total dependence on God and the scriptures. And, yet they continue to work. The farmers lose their crops but they keep on working in the fields, ploughing and sowing seeds, for they know that the land must be cultivated. They achieve a great balance in 'action and fate', based on the hope given by their religion.

The Hindus are different as they believe to have all the gods, goddesses, planets, constellations, zodiac in their palm. So, they believe in deeds. To keep themselves active, every morning they look at their palms and claim:

कराग्रे वसति लक्ष्मी करमध्ये सरस्वती।
करमूले स्थितो ब्रह्मा प्रातः कर दर्शनम्।।

Karãgre basati Laxmi karmadhye Saraswati
Karmoole sthito Brahma prãtah kar darshnam

(The Goddess of wealth resides at the tip of the fingers and the Goddess of learning in the middle of the palm and the Creator at the beginning of the palm, so one should look at the palm every morning.)

Hindus are really great. They are the descendents of great *rishis* who practised and taught their coming generations to salute the mother earth every morning before putting the feet on it:

समुद्रवसने देवि! पर्वतस्तनमंडले।
विष्णुपत्नी! नमस्तुभ्यं पादस्पर्शम् क्षमस्व मे।

Samudrabasanedevi! Parvatstanmandale
Vishnupatni! Namastubhyam pādsparsam chhamaswa me

They invite the gods at the start of a ritual and request them to return back to their respective abodes at the end of it. They pray for the purification of the outer self and the inner being: ***bāhyābhyantar shuchih***. Their greatness lies in the fact that they have numerous ways of salutation (*pranāyām vidhi*). We cannot discuss everything here but it is essential to draw the attention towards the most refined elements in the Hindu scriptures. It is the attitude and the intention that matters.

The Hindus are different because they believe that if and when they save the religion, only then the religion will save them: ***Dharmo rakshati rakshitah***.

So, all of them are religious at heart, even the stout atheists, the followers of *Chārwāk* and the *nihilists*. And all the Hindus are humanists first as the *rishis* and *devatas* did not tell them to be Hindus, they advised them to 'be human' *(manurbhawo)*.

OO

9

Purification and Bliss by Scriptures

आनो भद्राः क्रतवो यन्तु विश्वतः।

Āno bhadrāh kratavo yantu viswatah

(Let noble thoughts come to us from every side.)

The shortened and compact list of the selected scriptures is enough to give an insight into Human/Universal/Eternal Religion. The panorama of these divine and sublime works determine and specify the pious and essential duties of man towards God, Nature, Universe, Elements, other fellow beings and different creatures for co-existence, smooth running and continuation of life.

Conditioning of Body and Mind

Many things are essential for existence but two things are the most important and unfortunately are treated as the least significant. Both of them are, in a way, closely related and dependent on each other. The first one is closeness to Nature, while man is incessantly and with 'supersonic speed' running away from it. The conditioning of body and mind to be able to adapt to natural climate and calamity is required. The artificial abode (or construction plans on other planets) cannot be adequate protection, defence or armour. One cannot feel safe and get security when one is very far from Nature. Only Nature can fulfil the needs and protect the existing life in the form of plants, insects and animals against global warming, floods, tsunamis, tornadoes, tempests, lightning, fire, diseases and other calamities.

The Dark Side of Modern Life

Excessive artificial inventions and needless production on large scale are not required. There are two proofs that they are not needed. One is that they are luxury items and pollute everything including human mind and the other is that despite sensual and attractive advertisements and easy loans such unsold products are stuffed in each store. Through these products, we are destroying the ecology, atmosphere, exosphere and the all-important and protective ozone layer. Nothing can protect life on the earth if there is no ozone layer; today the ozone hole is 73 million kilometres wide.

The other most important thing is to reduce our needs which are growing and multiplying every day. Each 'new' invention has outdated its predecessor and made it useless.

The rejected garbage is a major problem for each household and a challenge to each metropolitan city and each mayor.

We must control our sensual and luxury-loving self. Contentment and frugality are two boons. We must work hard physically to allow the sweat to come out for health, fitness, freshness, fertility and pleasure. The basic needs cannot be compensated with the workouts in gyms. Outdoor games and physical labour are essential. Our indoor life and excess dependence on machinery has rendered us useless. The sooner we understand the better it is.

Man and his vital organs are becoming weaker and infertility is overpowering. The problem is really very acute. Our way of living, food preferences and other unnatural habits should be immediately and wisely replaced by those taught in the scriptures, because the scriptures were written after facing many such devastations. Why do you think, men and women of the country of *Gandharvas*, *Apasaras*, Vãtsyãyan, Chãrwak agreed to and are sincerely following the institution of marriage which was later on adopted by the whole world? The answer is simple. There was a time when almost each one was suffering from all the dirty and deadly venereal diseases, which were more dangerous than syphilis, gonorrhoea, and ultra-modern AIDS. There was no other option to make the sensual man a disciplined, obedient child to accept such bindings and limitations.

The universal ill-health and total dependence on medicine tells something. That 'something' must be heard intently and followed sincerely. Only then the doctors and medicines can be kept away and health, pleasure, happiness and fertility can return back in life.

What we can do

Now, we need to come closer both to Nature and the scriptures and follow them sincerely without raising unnecessary questions because we hardly know a thing. We do not know our physical body, the inner and outer organs; we do not know our family and our society, we are not sure of our needs and the purity of the things that we eat every day. Shakespeare claimed "Half of the world does not know how the other half lives." The modern man claims that the world has come into our drawing room yet we do not know how our family members, neighbours and others live. We are not sure about anything and often repeat that there is no guarantee of anything. On the other hand, all the scriptures are the collected wisdom of such sages who had up to ten thousand pupils at a time and were all the time in '*satsang*' (in mutual exchange of knowledge) and research, and they guarantee health, happiness, prosperity, purity, wisdom, emancipation and salvation. The world has foolishly chosen its ruin. Hence it is useless to search peace with the 'weapons of mass destruction', health from inaction, happiness from lust and pleasure from sensuality.

What our forefathers handed over to us safely, we have knowingly (despite repeated warning by modern wise men of the world) destroyed (rather ruined) it completely in the last 300 years of urbanisation, mechanisation and industrialisation. Thousands of years back, Manu clearly stated "Heavy machinery should not be manufactured". The statement simultaneously accepts the knowledge of heavy machinery and the dangers that they generate.

Manusmriti forbids the manufacture of great machines *"mahāyantrapravartanam"* (11/63). But man has been incessantly creating heavy machines and tools for the last 300 years. These unwise acts are bringing us closer to total extinction.

We must learn to live according to the scriptures, accept what nature gives and be contented; add whatever we can add to it in natural way and live with Nature to grow naturally strong, active, and health.

It is a fact that all are weak and ignorant at the time of birth. They grow. They develop. They acquire qualities. It is their willingness and inclination which makes them turn towards piety or crime. They do not fight against the worldly attractions (*Māyā*) that come their way and succumb to the allurements for they are weak inside and have not adapted themselves against hardships. Hence except for the pure persons and the criminals, most of the common men live and die unseen, unknown without a reasonable fight. Man was never so weak and dependent. One must try to become civilised, cultured, humane, purer, sublime and divine. The scriptures are there to help.

At present what we think to be prosperity is not prosperity because it kills happiness and destroys health; what we think to be food is not the healthy food, it is 'junk' food that sickens the organs and system. What we think to be entertainment is not entertainment but perversion.

काव्यशास्त्रविनोदेन कालोगच्छति धीमताम्।

Kavyashastravinoden kalogachhati dheemtam

(The best way to spend leisure time is in the delineation of poetry and scriptures.)

It is health that makes everything and every achievement possible and it is healthy entertainment that makes the soul grow. One must always remember that health is wealth.

See for yourself with your own eyes, look around the rural areas and people whom we despise as poor, illiterate, uncultured, ill-mannered and look down upon. These are the only healthy and happy people. The rest, including the most of the urban population is suffering acutely from numerous physical and mental diseases, and is somehow sustaining on medicines. They are neither getting physical pleasure nor mental peace, neither inner happiness nor material contentment. Despite the enormous wealth, luxurious living and immoral acts, the health and happiness is missing. Economic, social and moral crimes are rampant. There is no dearth of such criminals. It is the fall from heaven into artificially lighted corridors which actually lead to dark passages of hell.

Religion is discarded, belief is choked and faith is lost. All are living in the fatal darkness of a faithless, godless, irreligious and immoral world. People have no faith in themselves, their near and dear ones, in God, religion, government and diplomats. They lead a faithless and unhealthy life of demonic ideas and barbarous deeds. There is no life at all. All are following the same stale routine every day earning money and losing everything else. The loss of faith and hope is the greatest loss.

The scriptures will immediately fill you up with immense faith, bright hope for growth, creation and sustenance during the testing moments. Always remember, **"It is Faith that creates and the Hope that sustains"**.

FAITH and HOPE will bring and keep the scriptures open before you and make you live in the safe and secure lap of the mother earth, in natural settings under healthy shade and pure air. Do bring them closer and closely follow them for healthy and happy living. Do only those things which are pious with pure intention, dedication, devotion, surrender to the Almighty and follow Him and His dictates collected in scriptures to become free from endless pain, acute suffering, illusions and lust to lead a happy and healthy life on this beautiful, kind, compassionate, loving and all-giving mother Earth.

Life of a man was lighted vane,
Life of a man is the darkest lane.
Do not be a writer or pleader very great,
Live with love but not with hate.
Be a man loving and humane,
Not a beast cunning and profane.
Life of a man was lighted vane,
Life of a man is the darkest lane.
Do not be a trader or business tycoon,
Do not finish riches of the earth so soon.
Be her child stout and sane,
Grow not enmity, grow only grain.
Life of a man was lighted vane,
Life of a man is the darkest lane.
We cut ourselves with each green tree,
We are imprisoned with each bird free.
Deeds of men are really bane,
Humanity is in a state of wane.

Life of a man was lighted vane,
Life of a man is the darkest lane.
Whether the winter or the spring,
Music eternal flows from within.
Be the tune of showering rain,
Pure from beginning, and no stain.
Life of a man was lighted vane.
Life of a man is the darkest lane.

(From *'Self Unveiled'*)

Conclusion

The man must change his philosophy, psychology, preferences, work-schedule and working hours and way of living. He must achieve a balance. He must come out of his enclosed and stinking materialistic den, throw the prejudices and illusions away, accept the existence of each creature and plant essential and be a human being in reality and not remain simply a 'noun'.

The man of the modern world has been termed as 'Merchant of Death'. He will have to prove that he is not an arms-monger or a blood-thirsty creature. He will have to prove that he is the real human being with human feelings and nature and that he is the best and wisest creature that the Almighty created to safeguard life on earth. It must be proved by reasonable, wise, sincere, compassionate and human behaviour and deeds.

We can achieve it only by reading and following the Indian scriptures. The scriptures which were envisioned, collected, enshrined, followed and saved in India for all the human beings to get their way and develop their self for salvation. These are not Hindu scriptures, these are scriptures as Human Religion envisioned by the sages centuries and millenniums before the coinage of the word 'Hindu' or 'Hinduism' which was open enough to declare *Vasudhaiva kutumbakam*. The most important idea behind this two-word slogan is that it claims all human beings to be relatives which cannot be translated into universal brotherhood for they have not used the word 'brother' or 'friend'. They directly claim everyone to be relatives. It defined wholesome and unwholesome deeds in the most simple and straightforward way:

परोपकाराय पुण्याय पापाय परपीडनम्।

Paropkārāya punyāya pāpāya parpidanam

(To help others is piety, and to inflict injury to others is sin.)

Indian scriptures are the only scriptures that pray for 'all':

सर्वे भवन्तु सुखिनः सर्वे सन्तु निरामयाः।
सर्वे भद्राणि पश्यन्तु मा कश्चिद् दुःख भाग्भवेत्।।

Sarve bhawantu sukhinah sarve santu nirāmayāh
Sarve bhadrāni pashyantu mā kashchid dukh bhāg bhawet

Human religion must include within its fold all living and non-living beings to guard and save them. Man cannot exist after their extinction. He is because the Universe, the Cosmos, the earth and everything is there.

In that way, we can safely conclude that Hinduism is purely humanism and Hindu scriptures are the scriptures for all the human beings.

Purify your 'self' and get bliss and beatitude through the most ancient scriptures of the world written and compiled for the human beings.

असतो मा सद्गमय
तमसो मा ज्योतिर्गमय।

Asato mā sadgamaya
Tamaso mā jyotirgamaya

(From impurity awaken into purity, from darkness awaken into light.)

○○